Physical Plant Operations Handbook

PHYSICAL PLANT OPERATIONS HANDBOOK

K.L. Petrocelly
R.P.A., C.P.E.

Library of Congress Cataloging-in-Publication Data

Petrocelly, K. L. (Kenneth Lee), 1946-
    Physical plant operations handbook.

    Includes index.
1. Plant engineering--Handbooks, manuals, etc.
    I. Title.
    TS184.P43   1988   658.2   87-45736
    ISBN 0-88173-054-8

Published by The Fairmont Press, Inc.
700 Indian Trail
Lilburn, GA 30247

Printed in the United States of America

10 9 8 7 6 5 4 3 2

ISBN 0-88173-054-8   FP
ISBN 0-13-669235-4   PH

Distributed by Prentice-Hall, Inc.
A division of Simon & Schuster
Englewood Cliffs, NJ 07632

Prentice-Hall International (UK) Limited, London
Prentice-Hall of Australia Pty. Limited, Sydney
Prentice-Hall Canada Inc., Toronto
Prentice-Hall Hispanoamericana, S.A., Mexico
Prentice-Hall of India Private Limited, New Delhi
Prentice-Hall of Japan, Inc., Tokyo
Simon & Schuster Asia Pte. Ltd., Singapore
Editora Prentice-Hall do Brasil, Ltda., Rio de Janeiro

Dedication

This book is dedicated to Aimee and Anthony
for the hours they spent without me,
to Susan for the months she spent processing my words
and to Kenneth Jr. for the years he spent wondering
what I did for a living.

Preface

Whether you are called the facilities manager, plant engineer or by any other of the myriad titles conferred upon us, you can bet Sunday's doughnuts you will be called first and often when problems develop in the physical plant. Owing to technical advances and economic pressures in our field, our manifold duties have increased tremendously in recent years and the degree of accountability has risen proportionally. No longer are we the "guys in the basement" whose budget is first to be cut. At once we are expected to be architect, engineer, accountant and code interpreter. The hats we wear are as diversified as the problems confronting us. No other profession offers more unique challenges or sense of accomplishment and at the same time provides as many pitfalls or opportunities for failure than that of the Physical Plant Director. Knowledge and gut instinct are the brick and block with which we build our reputations. This work is meant to provide you with the footing on which to begin construction.

Kenneth Lee Petrocelly

Contents

Chapter 1
ASSUMING THE POSITION

They wined and dined you, gave you a copy of last year's prospectus, explained the organization's reporting mechanism and after a brief introduction to each of the department heads, installed you as the Plant Operations Director of a brand new building. Congratulations!

Go ahead. Sit back in that plush office chair, put your feet up and relax. After all, you've earned it . . . you know, all the hard work and schooling . . . etc. Feels good doesn't it?

Now I don't mean to burst your bubble and admittedly, the odds against such an occurrence are definitely on your side, but what would you do if the power to your building just went out? Call the power company? You probably wouldn't get an outside line due to the influx of calls you would be receiving from all the department heads you had met; for as far as they are concerned, you are the power company. What if the chillers shut down? What if your water supply is interrupted? What if . . .? Alright, you catch my drift, now what are you going to do about it?

Assuming your luck holds out and none of the before-mentioned predicaments befalls you during the remainder of your first day on the job, let me offer these suggestions. Put your feet on the floor, roll up your sleeves, plug in the coffeepot and call your supervisory staff in for a meeting.

GETTING ACQUAINTED

The next few hours you spend will be critical to your future success as director and may prove to be your most significant investment of time towards your understanding of the building's systems.

Once you've mustered the troops and supplied a mug of joe to every fist, let your hair down. Explain that the nature of the meeting will be informal and its purpose two fold; first, as an opportunity

1

to get you and the group acquainted with one another and second, to help familiarize yourself with the operation of the department. First impressions are important in establishing your authority and enlisting their support. By all means, tell them about your experiences and qualifications but be certain to recognize their worth and expertise. I'm a firm believer that, as go the sergeants, so goes the army. In the early going, these people are the ones you will be relying on to get you out of whatever jams you may get into.

You won't be able to gauge the productivity of this initial contact with your staff but good or bad, it will set the tone for your future dealings with them. You should thank your people for attending, express your elations for being blessed with such a proven team of professionals, determine who is best qualified to escort you on a plant tour and get on with it.

THE PLANT TOUR

After expressing your desire to survey every square foot of space under your charge, grab a notepad and put your ears on. You'll learn much more about the building and its systems by listening to your guide than by impressing him with how much you know. Besides, letting him do most of the talking not only allows you to take better notes but gives you an insight into his knowledge of the facility.

Opinions differ as to where to begin and how to proceed on an inspection tour. My preference is to start with the major equipment rooms and progress outward as the systems extend through the building. How you go about it personally probably doesn't matter, as long as you have become thoroughly oriented to the building and its systems by tour's end.

At this stage, the single best means of getting the information you are looking for is to ask questions—lots of them. But your inquiries should be abstract by nature since the statistical data you will need can probably be extracted from someones file cabinet. Your objective should be to gain a feel for the place, not an accounting of the number of bricks it took to construct it. Your interrogation should include but not be limited to:

- building and systems trouble spots
- recurring breakdowns of equipment

- frequency of power outages and surges
- nuisance tripping of system components
- capacity at which systems operate
- frequency and types of system interruptions
- contingencies for plant support during emergencies
- emergency power and uninterruptible power supplies
- the affect of outages/interruptions on departments

ORGANIZING THE PLANS

If you've taken the tour as I've prescribed it, you should be chock full of notes about now. Take a break. Go back to your office and grab a cup of coffee. It's okay to sit down in that plush chair now but don't put your feet up because you'll need the desk space to lay out the as-built drawings. Every new building comes replete with copies of the drawings used in its construction. Find the complete set on which all of the jurisdictional approvals appear and salt it away in a fire-proof vault for safe keeping. This set of plans should never be used for reference or written upon. It is your last bastion of defense in the building maintenance and renovation war.

Before you permanently store the approved plans in the archives, compare the several other copies of the drawings for accuracy against them. These will be used by you during the course of your work over the years to come. You should always maintain one clean and complete copy in your office and by no means should you ever give or lend it to anyone, not even the architect or CEO of your organization.

What comprises a complete set of drawings? Generally speaking, construction drawings come in a variety of sizes, often times depending on the scope of the project, governing body regulatory requirements, input from the ultimate owner operator and the preference of the firm charged with drawing up the plans. They may or may not include pictorial representations, schematics or a myriad of other data, but common to all is the fact that they are scaled-down graphic models of the real thing and can be interpreted by use of architects' and engineers' rulers. On the first or second sheet should be an index of the drawings in the set, similar to the table of contents of this book. Figure 1-1 is typical of what you might find.

INDEX OF DRAWINGS

CIVIL
C1.1 SITE GEOMETRY
C1.2 GRADING, DRAINAGE & SEDIMENT CONTROL
C1.3 SITE DETAILS

LANDSCAPE
L1.1 MASTER PLANTING PLAN
L1.2 DETAIL PLANTING PLAN
L1.3 PLANTING DETAILS

ARCHITECTURAL
A2.1 FIRST FLOOR PLAN
A2.2 SECOND & THIRD FLOOR PLANS
A3.1 EXTERIOR ELEVATIONS & ROOF PLANS
A4.1 WALL SECTIONS
A4.2 DETAILS
A4.3 DETAILS
A5.1 TYPICAL PATIENT ROOM PLANS
A6.1 CEILING PLAN - FIRST FLOOR
A6.2 CEILING PLAN - 2ND & 3RD FLOOR
A7.1 STAIRS & DETAILS
A7.2 ELEVATOR PLANS & DETAILS
A8.1 MISCELLANEOUS DETAILS
A8.2 MISCELLANEOUS DETAILS

INTERIORS
D2.1 FIRST FLOOR - FURNITURE PLAN
D2.2 2ND & 3RD FLOOR - FURNITURE PLAN

GRAPHICS
G2.1 EXTERIOR GRAPHICS
G2.2 1ST FLR - ACCENT WALLS & GRAPHICS
G2.3 2ND & 3RD FLR - ACCENT WALLS & GRAPHICS

STRUCTURAL
S1.1 FOUNDATION PLAN
S1.2 FOUNDATION PLAN
S1.3 FOUNDATION SECTIONS & DETAILS
S2.1 2ND FLR & LOW ROOF FRAMING PLAN
S2.2 2ND FLR & LOW ROOF FRAMING PLAN
S2.3 3RD FLR & LOW ROOF FRAMING PLAN
S3.1 STEEL SECTIONS & DETAILS
S4.1 SCHEDULES & TYPICAL DETAILS
S5.1 RIGID FRAME ELEVATIONS DETAILS

MECHANICAL
M0.1 H.V.A.C. SCHEDULES
M0.2 H.V.A.C. SCHEDULES
M2.1-123 H.V.A.C. 1ST FLR - SPLY, RTN &
    EXH DUCTS & PIPING
M2.1-1 FIRST FLOOR SUPPLY DUCTS
M2.1-2 H.V.A.C. 1ST FLR RETURN EXHAUST
M2.1-3 H.V.A.C. 1ST FLR PIPING
M2.2-123 H.V.A.C. 2ND & 3RD FLR -
    SPLY, RTN, EXH & PIPING
M2.2-1 H.V.A.C. 2ND & 3RD FLR - SUPPLY
M2.2-2 H.V.A.C. 2ND & 3RD FLR -
    RTN & EXH DUCTS
M2.2-3 H.V.A.C. 2ND & 3RD FLR PIPING
M2.3 H.V.A.C. ROOF PLAN
M3.1 H.V.A.C. POWERHOUSE & EQUIP RMS
M5.1 H.V.A.C. CONTROLS & WIRING
M6.1 H.V.A.C. DETAILS
M6.2 H.V.A.C. DETAILS

PLUMBING
P1.1 SITE PLAN - PLUMBING
P2.1 UNDERGROUND PLUMBING
P2.2 FIRST FLOOR - PLUMBING
P2.3 2ND & 3RD FLR - PLUMBING

P3.1 POWERHOUSE
P4.1 WASTE & WATER RISER SCHEMATICS
P6.1 SCHEDULES & DETAILS
P6.2 DETAILS
P6.3 DETAILS & SEWER PROFILE

ELECTRICAL
E0.1 SCHEDULE SHEET
E1.1 SITE PLAN
E2.1 1ST FLR LIGHTING
E2.2 1ST FLR POWER & SYSTEMS
E2.3 2ND & 3RD FLR LIGHTING
E2.4 2ND & 3RD FLR POWER & SYSTEMS
E3.1 POWERHOUSE LIGHTING
E3.2 POWERHOUSE POWER
E3.3 ROOF PLAN
E4.1 POWER DISTRIBUTION DIAGRAM
E5.1 ELECTRICAL WIRING DIAGRAM &
    CONSOLE ELEVATIONS
E5.2 ELECTRICAL DIAGRAMS & LEGEND

Figure 1-1. Section and Sheet Index, Building Plans

As you can see, the drawings provide you with a wealth of information that can be gleaned from them in the relative comfort of your office without ever having to leave your desk.

The CIVIL section usually shows the acreage, land boundaries and contour, elevation, building location, and parking lot layouts.

The LANDSCAPE section lists the botanical and common names of plantings used, assigns their location and prescribes the methods used in their placement.

the ARCHITECTURAL section shows and identifies the compartmentalization of the interior of the building and stairwells. It almost always has a great number of detail drawings to refer to.

The INTERIORS section provides you with the initial planned layout of the fixtures and furniture that are to be included as part of the project package.

The GRAPHICS section depicts the types and positioning of the signage used in and around the building and determines the location of accent walls within the structure.

The STRUCTURAL section includes foundation and roof framing layouts, rigid frame elevations and method of attachment details.

The MECHANICAL section usually provides schedules indicating the sizes and capacities of all the mechanical devices and components used throughout the building. Air supply valves and duct sizes and locations are available on the prints, as well as pictorial details of powerhouse equipment.

The PLUMBING section shows the location of the water supply and waste and storm drain mains located outside of the building. It also shows the water riser and distribution lines and valves, locations and sizes as well as the drain system piping and clean-out locations inside of the building.

The ELECTRICAL section identifies the location of the light standards and electrical hookups of ancillary equipment found outside of the building and provides data on all electric circuits from the point where service enters the building, through the main and secondary distribution panels, including lighting and motor control panels.

As indicated previously, the index example is just that; an example. The drawings may and usually do include much more information than the representative sampling supplied by Figure 1-1. They may include such things as sprinkler systems or communications schematics, kitchen layouts, door and casework schedules or other data or specifications that are integral to the project.

TRACING OUT THE SYSTEMS

Armed with the plans and a fresh impression of the building and its equipment rooms in your mind, now is a good time to trace out the major components of each of your systems.

Referring to Figure 1-1, at a minimum, review sheets P1.1, P2.1, P3.1, P4.1 and P6.3 of the plumbing section and sheets E0.1, E1.1, E3.1, E3.2 and especially E4.1 of the electrical section, paying particular attention to the location of the main and secondary main shut-offs and how interruption of service from those points will affect operations downstream. In alleviating a bad situation, although shutting the main valve or switch may turn the trick, you might well cause more problems to manifest themselves than if you had shut down a branch main closer to the problem area.

While reviewing the plans, if they don't readily identify the area serviced, it is often a good idea to use the transparent mylar copy of the architectural drawing as an overlay when interpreting your systems drawings, assuming they fit up by scale. This will enable you to assimilate how the utilities progress through and service the identified user compartments.

Whatever you do, don't put the plans away until you are confident that you can quarterback the situation, should a dire emergency befall your operations.

CALLING IT A DAY

Well it certainly was an exhausting day for you, wasn't it? Look how much you've learned in such a short period of time. But don't leave to beat the rush-hour traffic just yet. If that unlikely problem does arise, it will probably take more than your new-found knowledge and good intentions to resolve it.

Aside from the building specifications manuals that should accompany you home for your evenings' reading pleasure, your briefcase should contain the following:

- an organizational chart showing the names and telephone numbers of the persons filling those positions and their reporting order

- a copy of the firm's emergency contingency plan

- the names and telephone numbers of all persons reporting to you
- a complete listing of emergency telephone numbers of regulatory, municipal and vendor contacts
- a copy of the current workers' schedule for your department

Now you're not armed to the hilt against all possible catastrophies, but you should be considered at least moderately prepared to take on the difficulties you might more likely encounter, such as nuisance calls for routine maintenance items and false alarms.

Let your people know how to contact you if you're needed before tomorrow, lock up, drive carefully and I'll see you in the a.m.

Chapter 2
ESTABLISHING A ROUTINE

Good Morning! So your night was uneventful? That's great. And the birds were chirping outside of your sunshine-drenched bedroom? That's marvelous. But if the sun was shining when you left for work, it's your tires that should have been chirping in your rush to get here. You should have downed your second cup of office brew and been well into your working day by now. Apparently no one has informed you, but in this job you are married to your work and the honeymoon ended after your pre-employment dinner with the CEO. Shall we begin day two?

THE KEY TO SUCCESS

Every job has its rituals and routines and ours is no exception. The difference being that we are afforded more flexibility in their choosing due to the diverse nature of our role within the organization. Of all the brass hats in the place, we are the most individually accountable members of management. No other position in your facility has as much direct contact with all the others, regardless of their stations. Our visibility demands that we interact daily and at times even hourly with a wide variety of personalities.

Good communications between yourself and all persons within or having dealings with your organization are imperative if you are to succeed in your position. Always take the opportunity to converse with anyone affiliated in any way with you as representative of your organization and never speak ill of it. Bearing that thought in mind, let's establish a routine.

FIRST THINGS FIRST

Each morning, after reviewing the night shift's operating logs, make it a point to meet informally with your supervisory staff to discuss the prior night's events, current issues confronting your department and your expectations of what is to occur throughout the remainder of the day. Allow them to input their thoughts and opinions to you and by no means let the meeting end until everyone has a clear understanding of the information conveyed.

Check your office for any messages that may have been received during your absence and respond to them immediately, regardless of the importance you may place on them personally. What appears to be an insignificant item to you will probably be considered an extreme predicament to the requester and there is always the possibility that the seriousness of the problem was not conveyed by the message taker. The idea here isn't to promptly resolve the problem, although that would be a definite plus, rather it is to apprise the sender that you are aware of the problem and will take action on it. Whether the action only entails adding it to the work order system for routine attention or calls for a more concerted effort on your part, you should be construed as being in control of the situation.

Once the work has been accomplished, always make it a point to inform the sender that his request has been honored. Often times, even though the problem has been corrected, the initiator of the request is unaware of the fact and assumes that the work still needs to be done.

LOOKING FOR TROUBLE

Your people are on the job and you've taken care of everyones concerns. Now is a good time to take an impromptu tour of the plant. You should make an effort to walk through the facility at least once a day, noting any obvious discrepancies and once a week, armed with a clipboard and inspection forms to ferret out less noticeable maladies that could surface as major concerns further down the road.

Since you are alone this trip and still feeling your way around, why not take the long walk. Go ahead; pick up the clipboard. I'll supply the forms. Even if you get lost you'll appear as though you know what you're doing.

As I stated in Chapter 1, everybody has their own preference as to how they proceed through the plant, so use the forms that follow in whatever order you desire. I'll see you back at the office.

PHYSICAL PLANT EVALUATION

ROOF		BUILDING	AREA

ITEM	ACCEPTABLE		REMARKS
	YES	NO	
DOORS, LOCKS, LATCHES			
SKYLIGHTS			
HATCHES, LADDERS			
PARAPET WALLS			
PENTHOUSE WALLS			
WALKBOARDS			
PLATFORMS, DECKS			
ROOF MEMBRANES			
STONE DISTRIBUTION			
VENT PIPING, STACKS			
FLASHING			
BUILDING JOINTS			
DRAINS			
LIGHTNING RODS, CABLES			
TRANSMISSION LINES			
ANTENNA INSTALLATION			
WARNING LIGHTS			
SIGNAGE			
EXHAUST FANS, HOUSINGS			
A/C UNITS			
DUCT WORK INSULATION			
COOLING TOWERS			
EQUIPMENT ROOMS			
AIR INTAKES			
HELIPAD			
SURVEYOR		DATE	

Figure 2-1. Roof Inspection Form

PHYSICAL PLANT EVALUATION

POWER PLANT		BUILDING	AREA

ITEM	ACCEPTABLE		REMARKS
	YES	NO	
FUEL LEAKS			
OIL LEAKS			
WATER LEAKS			
STEAM LEAKS			
AIR LEAKS			
SUMP PUMP OPERATION			
FLOOR DRAINS			
DOORS, STAIRS, LADDERS			
WALKWAYS, GRATINGS			
PIPE HANGERS			
EXPANSION JOINTS			
PIPING INSULATION			
EQUIPMENT INSULATION			
AIR LOUVRES, FILTERS			
ROOM LIGHTING			
INDICATOR LIGHTS			
CHEMICAL FEED PUMPS			
WATER PRESSURE			
STACK TEMPERATURES			
UNUSUAL NOISES			
EXCESSIVE VIBRATION			
STAND BY FUEL			
CHEMICAL PAR LEVELS			
PARTS INVENTORY			
ANCILLARY ROOMS			
SURVEYOR			DATE

Figure 2-2. Power Plant Inspection Form

PHYSICAL PLANT EVALUATION

FLOOR ROUNDS		BUILDING	AREA

ITEM	ACCEPTABLE		REMARKS
	YES	NO	
DOOR CLOSURE, HARDWARE			
WINDOWS, BLINDS			
WALL COVERINGS			
FLOOR COVERINGS			
CEILING TILES			
LIGHT FIXTURES			
ROOM LIGHTING			
EXIT LIGHTS			
ELECTRICAL PANELS			
EXTENSION/POWER CORDS			
SIGNAGE			
WATER FOUNTAINS			
ROOM TEMPERATURE			
AIR DIFFUSERS/RETURNS			
FIRE HAZARDS			
TRIPPING HAZARDS			
JAGGED EDGES			
FIRE EXTINGUISHERS			
WATER LEAKS			
REST ROOMS			
KITCHENETTES			
STORAGE ROOMS			
JANITOR CLOSETS			
GENERAL APPEARANCE			
SURVEYOR		DATE	

Figure 2-3. Activity Areas Inspection Form.

PHYSICAL PLANT EVALUATION

LOBBY/STAIRWELL

BUILDING	AREA

ITEM	ACCEPTABLE		REMARKS
	YES	NO	
GLASS FRONTS			
DOOR OPERATION, LOCKS			
WEATHERSTRIPPING			
THRESHOLDS			
ENTRY/EXIT DEVICES			
WALK MATS			
WALL COVERINGS			
FLOOR COVERINGS			
CEILING TILES			
LIGHTING			
SIGNAGE			
WAYS OF TRAVEL			
ELEVATOR BANKS			
GENERAL APPEARANCE			
DOOR CLOSURE/HARDWARE			
HANDRAILS			
TREADS			
LIGHTING			
VISION PANELS			
STANDPIPES			
FLOOR IDENTIFICATION			
ROOF HATCH			
OVERALL APPEARANCE			
SURVEYOR		DATE	

Figure 2-4. Lobby & Stairwell Inspection Form

PHYSICAL PLANT EVALUATION

GARAGE/EXTERIOR	BUILDING	AREA

ITEM	ACCEPTABLE		REMARKS
	YES	NO	
STRUCTURAL INTEGRITY			
TRAVEL SURFACES			
LIGHTING			
WATER LEAKAGE			
SIGNAGE			
FIRE PROTECTION			
ELEVATORS			
TOLL BOOTHS			
HEATING SYSTEMS			
STRIPING			
GENERAL APPEARANCE			
MARQUEE			
BUILDING SKIN			
REAR EXIT DOORS			
SIGNAGE			
LIGHT STANDARDS			
PARKING AREAS			
LOADING ZONE			
SIDEWALKS, DRIVES			
GROUNDS MAINTENANCE			
LANDSCAPING			
FIRE LANES/HYDRANTS			
PLAZA AREAS			
SURVEYOR		DATE	

Figure 2-5. Garage & Exterior Inspection Form.

PHYSICAL PLANT EVALUATION

DEPARTMENT		BUILDING	AREA

ITEM	ACCEPTABLE		REMARKS
	YES	NO	
COMMUNICATIONS SYSTEMS			
CENTRAL TIME SYSTEM			
FIRE WARNING SYSTEM			
SECURITY CAMERAS			
ELECTRICAL ROOMS			
MECHANICAL ROOMS			
VEHICLES			
GROUNDS EQUIPMENT			
SHOP EQUIPMENT			
MACHINE GUARDS			
SAFETY EQUIPMENT			
FIRE EXTINGUISHERS			
FIRST AID SUPPLIES			
TASK LIGHTING			
SIGNAGE			
PARTS ROOM			
TOOL CRIB			
STORAGE ROOM			
BULLETIN BOARD			
TIME CLOCK			
WORK SCHEDULE			
SUGGESTION BOX			
EMPLOYEE DRESS			
OFFICE SUPPLIES			
OVERALL APPEARANCE			
SURVEYOR		DATE	

Figure 2-6. Department Inspection Form

KEEPING CURRENT

Welcome back. You found a few problems didn't you? Don't fret over it; nine times out of ten, you will. If there are no urgent problems to handle, save the list for your staff meeting in the morning. Your maintenance supervisor can incorporate it into the work order system tomorrow. You have more pressing matters to attend to before everyone finds out that you're here.

During the lull between telephone calls is a good time to brush up on your reading. How's that? Sure, but while I'm pouring you a cup, pull these files out of your cabinet:

- architects statement of construction
- building and equipment inspection file
- equipment operating certificates
- departmental budget package
- departmental policy and procedures manual

Here's your coffee. You say you found everything but the P and P's? That's okay, you'll be rewriting most of them later anyway. Well, enjoy yourself. You'll be lucky to get through all the material without interruption. Later your reading time should include more palatable fare, such as trade journals, seminar handouts, technical manuals and a variety of correspondence, but for now, it's simply a matter of digesting as much existing data as you can ingest.

I imagine you're growing weary of my banter about now so I'm going to split. After all, you're the boss and I'm sure you can take it from here.

Enjoy your day and call me if you need me.

Chapter 3

THE EQUIPMENT INVENTORY

You just couldn't get along without me, could you? Both of your boilers are down, so here I am and yes, I knew you weren't a boilerman and you've only been here for two days and after all you can't be expected to know everything and . . .

Stop snivelling. It never got below 50 degrees last night and no harm was done. Hit the resets on the low-water fuel cut outs. Your water level in both units was low because you lost the coupler on the feed water pump. Don't worry, I switched pumps and you're back in business.

How's that? Sure, if you put a pot of coffee on, I'll be happy to describe what you should look for in the equipment rooms. We can start right here.

BOILERS

By strict definition, a boiler is a closed vessel in which liquid is converted into vapor by conducting heat from a heat source through a heating surface and into the liquid. In most cases, the liquid is water and the vapor is steam. Although the definition above implies that a boiling action must take place in the vessel, it is commonly accepted that high temperature hot water units are referred to as boilers, as well.

The uses of boilers are only limited by the imagination of the systems designers and the needs of the physical plant in which they do duty. The steam they produce can be used for melting ice and snow from walkways and drives, sterilizing instruments, cleaning engine blocks or a number of other functions, but in a modern physical plant setting, they are most commonly utilized to provide comfort heating, humidification and production of domestic hot water supplies.

The boilers most often associated with heating plants are the FIRE TUBE, WATER TUBE and SECTIONAL types. Each of these operates on the same principle of heat transfer and can be used for either steam or hot water service and in high or low pressure applications, depending on their design. The major differences in their construction are in the proximity of the water to the heat source and the materials from which they are made.

FIRE TUBE boilers (Figure 3-1) are made of steel and manufactured in sizes up to 15,000 pounds of steam per hour with maximum allowable working pressures up to 250 pounds per square inch. Physically, they come in a variety of sizes and configurations and are principally used for heating systems. Low pressure units are limited to 15 psig for steam service and a maximum of 160 psig and 250 degrees Fahrenheit for water service. Their large water storage capacities are useful in controlling the affects of sudden load fluctuations, but considerable time can be lost in bringing them up to operating pressure from a cold start. Heat exchange is accomplished in these units by passing hot gasses through metal tubes which are surrounded by water.

Figure 3-1. Fire Tube Boiler. (Courtesy of Cleaver-Brooks.)

WATER TUBE boilers (Figure 3-2) are made of steel and are used when large steam generating capacities and high pressures are required. As a rule, they have better efficiency ratings than do fire tube boilers but cost more to install initially. Heat exchange takes place in the generating tube bank, wherein water is passed through metal tubes which are surrounded by hot gasses from the heat source.

Figure 3-2a. Water Tube Boiler. (Courtesy of Cleaver-Brooks.)

Figure 3-2b. Water Tube Boiler.
(Courtesy of Cleaver-Brooks.)

SECTIONAL boilers (Figure 3-3) are made of cast iron and are used primarily for low pressure applications of 15 psig for steam service and 30 psig for water service. Operating and maintenance costs are much lower than that for fire tube and water tube boilers but initial erection costs can be high since fit up and assembly are usually performed on the premises. Heat is transferred in this unit by directing hot gases between cast iron sections in which water is contained.

Figure 3-3. Sectional Boiler. (Courtesy of Cleaver-Brooks.)

BOILER SYSTEMS

Just as no man is an island, a boiler cannot properly function independent of support from external sources. The activation of five separate, though interrelated systems is necessary before any boiler can be safely operated. These systems provide feed water, fuel, combustion air, pressure regulation and safe control of the unit.

A malfunction within any of the systems can end in disaster. If the unit suffers a low water condition resulting from loss of feed water during the night, your boiler may resemble a giant sinker in the morning and unless you're fishing for whales . . . If it loses combustion air, you might lose your boiler operator when he lights off the furnace, due to the accumulation of unspent fuel in the fire box. Scary, huh? Okay, doom-sayer dribble aside, let's continue.

In a typical installation:

The FEED WATER and CONDENSATE RETURN SYSTEM has the double duty of returning system condensate for reuse as feed water and providing makeup, from an alternate source, for water lost during the water-steam-water cycle. Separation of the condensate from the steam is accomplished by the use of steam traps located upstream of the feed water system. Before being returned to the boiler, the condensate is usually stored in a vacuum tank, condensate receiver, deaerating feed water heater or some combination of these, wherein the make-up feed water is normally added and preheating, deaeration and preliminary chemical treatment of the water takes place. From there, the feed water passes through the valves and controls located along the feed water trane before being introduced into the boiler, by pump or injector, at a pressure above that at which the unit operates.

The FUEL system can be simple or elaborate depending on the type of fuel used and the conditioning it is subjected to. The three types of boilers mentioned earlier can be modified to burn many kinds of fuels but in a physical plant setting such as ours, they are generally limited to burning natural or bottled gas, oil, coal to a lesser degree, or some combination of these. Natural gas is by far the cleanest burning fuel and causes the least amount of maintenance to be performed on the boiler. It doesn't require a pump or storage tank and if purchased from a utility, you are almost guaranteed an unexhaustible supply. Oil must be delivered, stored in tanks which much be sounded, analyzed and treated when stored for long periods of time, preheated depending on the grade, strained and filtered, pumped through a recirculating system and cleaned from the boilers' heating surfaces in the form of soot and carbon deposits, on a regular basis. Coal must be delivered with an attached analysis sheet of its constituents, washed, stored in bins, milled depending on its size and the system design, transported on conveyors, introduced into the furnace by a mechanical stoker and cleaned from the combustion chamber in the form of soot on the heating surfaces or ash from the fuel bed, which must be disposed of.

The DRAFT system supplies air for the combustion process and removal of unspent fuel vapors and exhaust gasses. Furnaces are fired using the principle of fluid convection or natural circulation, which is dependent on the relative densities of the heated to the unheated air or by mechanical means. Mechanical draft is provided by forced draft fans which blow air through the combustion chamber, induced draft fans which draw the air through or by using a combination of the two fans.

The PRESSURE system issues forth steam under its own power or hot water by pump into the main discharge line, through the header and to the load. On steam boilers, pressure is controlled by the operating control which lights off and shuts down the burner, on pressure, within the boilers' adjusted operating range.

The SAFETY system incorporates all the devices and consideration that go together to ensure safe operation of equipment. It is the safety valve and the operator who periodically tests it, the flame safeguard controls and the electrician who checks them, the safety interlocks and the mechanic who maintains them. In other words, safe operation of the unit is not guaranteed by its design, nor should it be taken for granted. The most important cog in the safety wheel is constant vigilance by a competent person.

BOILER TRIM

To most people, trim is an unattainable aspiration to fit their bodies to their accessories. To boilers, the accessories fitted to their bodies are referred to as trim. I know. I know. Shall we proceed?

Trim items on a boiler are all the elements integral and attached to the boiler proper, including its design features and all of the safety, monitoring and operating controls which make it a complete unit. As no two units are identical, I will cite only those trim items most commonly found on the types of boilers we have been discussing.

BOTTOM BLOW DOWN VALVES — Used for draining the boiler for cleaning, inspection and repair, controlling high water conditions and carryover, lowering chemical concentrations and removing sediment and sludge

BURNER CONTROL PANEL — Contains the combustion safety interlocks and cycling controls which provide for safe operation of the burner

FEED WATER REGULATOR — Opens and closes the feed water valve or starts or stops the feed water pump while monitoring the water level in the boiler

GAUGE GLASS — Visually indicates the level of water in a steam boiler

HANDHOLE — Inspection opening in the boiler shell having minimum allowable dimensions of two and three-quarters by three and one-half inches

HIGH LIMIT CONTROL — A device used to shut down the burner when the normal operating pressure has been exceeded

LOW WATER FUEL CUT OFF — Shuts off the supply of fuel to the burner when the water level in the boiler falls below the lowest setting on the feed water regulator

MAIN DISCHARGE VALVE — The first valve on the discharge line, located between the top of the boiler and the header, which is used for isolating a unit in a battery while maintaining the others under pressure

MANHOLE — Inspection opening in the boiler shell large enough to allow an average sized person to enter it for the purpose of cleaning, inspection or repair of the unit, having minimum allowable dimensions of eleven by fifteen inches or ten by sixteen inches for elliptical openings and fifteen inches diameter for circular openings

OBSERVATION PORT — Allows the operator to observe the flame in the fire box, enabling him to make adjustments to the burner

OVERPRESSURE VALVES — Valves which are used to release the pressure generated by a boiler when it exceeds the maximum allowable working pressure or design pressure of the unit. In steam service they are referred to as safety valves. In hot water service they are referred to as relief valves

PRESSURE GAUGE — Indicates the pressure inside the boiler in units of pounds per square inch

STACK THERMOMETER — Indicates the temperature of the gasses leaving the unit

WATER COLUMN — A device fitted with try cock valves that serves as a secondary means for checking the water level in a steam boiler. It also acts as a cushion against the turbulent action of the boiling water in the unit, so that the gauge glass will provide a truer indication of the water level in the boiler

I can see that all this talk about boilers has warmed you to further discussions of your equipment inventory so let me give you the cold facts of our next topic.

AIR CONDITIONING SYSTEMS

Ask ten people what an air conditioner does and more than likely, ten of them will say that it makes cold air. That is tantamount to saying that an automobile engine runs because you turn the key in the ignition or that telephones ring because they have bells in them. Simply put, air conditioning is a process whereby we condition the air. Depending on the desired result, air can be manipulated such that its temperature, humidity, volume, pressure, quality and distribution can be controlled simultaneously, through the use of present-day air conditioning equipment.

The end use determines how air conditioning systems are referred to and establishes the parameters for their operation. If a system is used to prepare air for use in an industrial setting, such as a microchip manufacturing plant or a chocolate factory, it is a process conditioner. If it is used to prepare air for human habitation, it is a comfort conditioner. It's the latter type of system that is more often encountered in the building plant, so I will limit my discussion to it. Comfort conditioning systems are classified as either absorption or compression types, depending on the method used to circulate refrigerant through the machine that forms the heart of the system.

In absorption machines (Figure 3-4), water is cycled as a refrigerant by subjecting it to a high vacuum, in the evaporator, where it is boiled off at relatively low temperatures by absorbing the heat transmitted by the evaporator coil. The water vapor flows into the absorber where lithium bromide spray absorbs it due to its great affinity for water. The diluted lithium bromide is reconcentrated by heating it in a generator where the water is boiled out of solution.

The water vapor flows into a condenser where it returns to a liquid state, then flows back to the evaporator and the concentrated lithium bromide is returned to the absorber, completing the cycle. Absorption units have no moving parts except for their solution, vacuum and refrigerant pumps and a couple of solenoid valves. They run quietly and are relatively maintenance free.

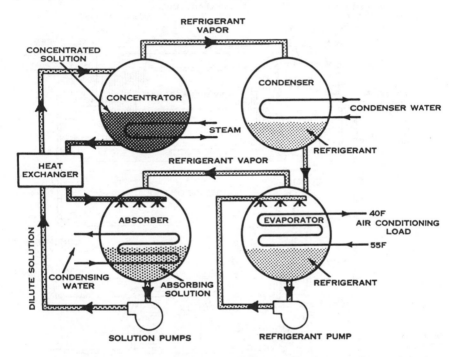

Figure 3-4. Flow Diagram of Absorption Refrigeration System. (Reproduced by permission of the Trane Company, La Crosse, Winconsin.)

Outside of their effect, compression machines bear no resemblance to their absorber cousins. In compression machines (Figure 3-5), low pressure liquid refrigerant is boiled off by the load heat transmitted in the evaporator, then flows through the suction line before entering the compressor as a low pressure gas. Here it is compressed into a high pressure gas and sent to a condenser, where the heat gained in the evaporator and from the action of compression is dissipated, returning the gas to liquid form, at high pressure. The high pressure liquid is then fed through a metering device to the evaporator and the cycle is completed. Air conditioning compressors are classed as either reciprocating or centrifugal depending on their method of compression. Both types are noisy and the reciprocating compressor can be a considerable source of problems if the unit is not properly maintained.

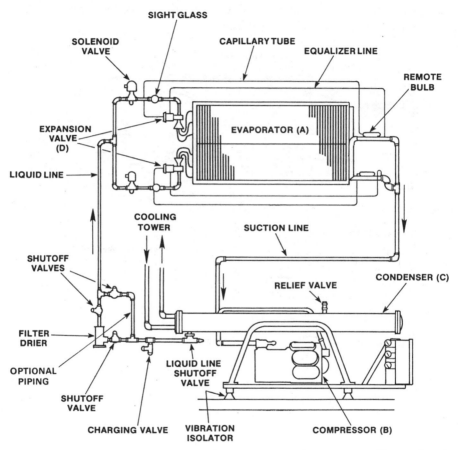

Figure 3-5. Flow Diagram of Compression Refrigeration System. (Reproduced by permission of the Trane Company, La Crosse, Wisconsin.)

AUXILIARY EQUIPMENT

Since no two physical plants are layed out exactly the same, any attempt to compile a comprehensive list of the support equipment one might find in a building's mechanical rooms would prove futile, at best. The kinds and types of equipment available staggers the imagination and its selection, installation, care and repair can challenge the abilities of even the most competent of plant managers. So I'll keep it simple.

Aside from the two major system components we have already addressed, the bulk of the items to be found in the plant can be broken down into three categories; electric motors, pumps and compressors, and pressure vessels.

ELECTRIC MOTORS have become so common place in the modern world that, not only do people take them for granted, they sometimes aren't even conscious of their existence. If asked, the average Joe couldn't tell you how many motors he has in his own house. Think about it. Can you list the motors you would find in yours? Unless you have electric baseboard or steam heat, you probably have an electric motor driving your forced-air blower or water pump. You will find motors in your clocks, phonograph turntables, washer and dryer, freezer compartment and driving the compressor in your refrigerator, the blender, the rotisserie in your microwave, your electric shaver, power tools, fans and air conditioners and even directional antenna rotors. The point isn't that people are unaware of their surroundings but that electric motors have become so dependable, there is no need for people to bother with them except when they fail or unless they do duty in a plant operations setting. But now we're broaching the subject of preventive maintenance and that's a topic that will be tackled more specifically later in the book.

Electric motors are simply machines that convert electrical energy into mechanical action. They come in sizes from fractional to over 20,000 horsepower and their uses are practically limitless. Depending on their design, they can be powered by either alternating or direct current and are wired for single- or poly-phase service.

In the plant, three-phase induction motors (Figure 3-6) are the ones you will more frequently encounter. Essentially they are constructed with two main parts; the stator and the rotor. The stator is a hollow, cylindrical, laminated core to which the stator windings are attached. As its name implies, it is the stationary part of the motor. Its function is to supply the magnetic field which causes the rotor to turn. The rotor is the rotating part of the motor and comes in two basic designs; the wound rotor or the squirrel cage rotor. The wound rotor consists of a three-phase winding attached to laminated slots, similar to the one in the stator. The squirrel cage rotor is constructed of conducting bars that are shorted together by welding them to copper end rings.

Figure 3-6. Three-phase Induction Motor. (Courtesy of Baldor Electric Company.)

Item No.	Part Name and Description
1	Front Endplate
2	Thru Bolts
3	Eye Bolt
4	Wound Stator Assembly
5	Rotor and Shaft Assembly
6	Pulley Endplate
7	Retainer Ring Bolts
8	Conduit Box Adapter
9	Conduit Box
10	Box Lid
11	Wavy Washer

It is imperative that the plant manager become familiar with the horsepower, voltages, phasing and types of motors scattered throughout his plant and that he closely monitors their operation and care.

PUMPS are devices used to transport liquids from one point to another. The three main classes of pumps found in use today are best described by their action. They are reciprocating, rotary and centrifugal.

Reciprocating pumps (Figure 3-7) draw liquid into cylinders from which it is pushed into a discharge line by the use of pistons. These kinds of pumps are referred to as positive displacement pumps since a given quantity of liquid is discharged with each stroke of the piston. Reciprocators are well suited for high pressure applications.

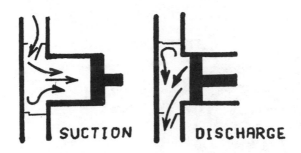

Figure 3-7. Reciprocating Pump; Suction & Discharge.

Rotary pumps (Figure 3-8) incorporate gears, screws or sliding vanes that draw liquid into openings between their teeth, threads or vanes which force the liquid into the discharge line in a given quantity for each revolution of the shaft. They are also positive displacement pumps and are used primarily as a source of power in hydraulic systems.

Figure 3-8. Rotary Pump Action.

Centrifugal pumps (Figure 3-9) draw water into the center of an impeller which flings the water into a volute by using the centrifugal force generated by its rotation. The spiral-shaped volutes progressive expansion in size reduces the velocity of the liquid and creates a static pressure in the discharge line. Due to the construction of this style pump, some slippage of the liquid is encountered and its capacity at constant speed can only be relied upon to deliver a maximum pressure based on its design, unlike the positive displacement pumps mentioned earlier. Centrifugal pumps are the most commonly used for general physical plant service.

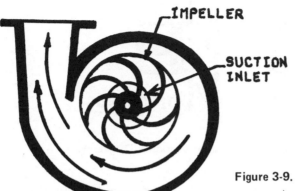

Figure 3-9. Centrifugal Pump Action.

COMPRESSORS (Figure 3-10) are nothing more than pumps used to pressurize and transport gasses. Like pumps, they have three main classes; reciprocating, rotary and centrifugal. The principles of operation for compressors is virtually the same as for pumps, except that whereas gasses as a rule can be compressed, liquids are, for all practical purposes, noncompressible.

PRESSURE VESSELS are closed containers, the contents of which exerts evenly distributed pressure, above a perfect vacuum, on their internal surfaces. They come in two varieties; fired and unfired.

Fired pressure vessels (Figure 3-11) are heated by gasses issuing from the combustion of a fuel such as natural gas or oil. Although there are many applications in industry for this device, in the physical plant, their use is generally limited to heating water.

Unfired pressure vessels can be heated or unheated. Heated vessels often perform the same work as fired vessels except that they do not derive their heat from the combustion process. Their heat source is usually waste heat gasses, steam or electrical resistance. Unheated vessels are mainly containers in which fluids are stored. Unfired pressure vessels (Figure 3-12) can be found throughout the plant in the form of heat exchangers, and air, oil or water storage tanks.

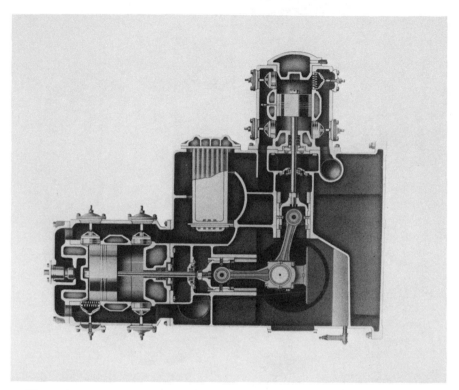

Figure 3-10a. Reciprocating Air Compressor. (Courtesy of Ingersoll-Rand.)

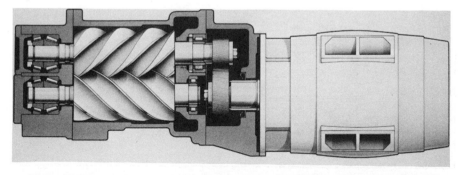

Figure 3-10b. Rotary Screw Air Compressor. (Courtesy of Ingersoll-Rand.)

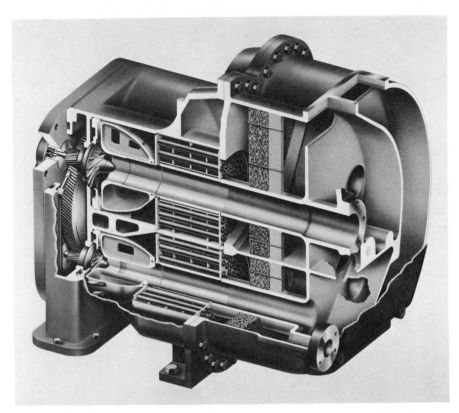

Figure 3-10c. Centrifugal Air Compressor. (Courtesy of Ingersoll-Rand.)

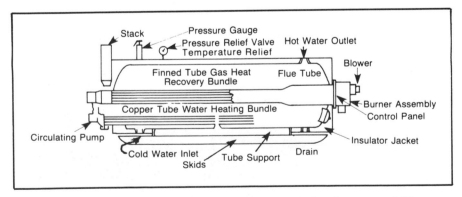

Figure 3-11. Fired Pressure Vessel. (Courtesy: Building Owners and Managers Institute.)

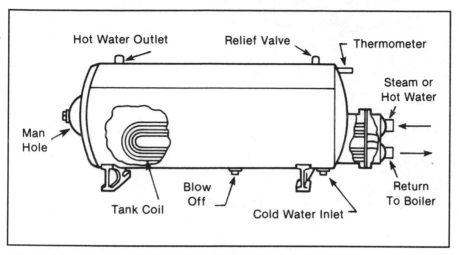

Figure 3-12. Unfired Pressure Vessel. (Courtesy: Building Owners and Managers Institute.)

By no means have I covered all the information you need to sit for a Stationary Engineers exam, but then what more can you expect for a cup of coffee? You'll read enough about equipment over the coming years to literally establish your own library. In the mean time, I suggest you take some time to review your operating manuals.

Chapter 4

TROUBLESHOOTING EQUIPMENT PROBLEMS

Now that you know what to look for in your mechanical spaces, let's explore some things to look out for in your mechanisms. No device or system has ever been designed or installed that doesn't have the potential to malfunction. Time alone predisposes them to failure.

THE TROUBLESHOOTER

Troubleshooting malfunctioning equipment and systems is a more complex process than the corrective maintenance measures used in repairing items whose problems are more obviously manifested. Therefore, it is important that you choose the proper person to designate as troubleshooter in your physical plant. He must be a cut above the average mechanic and possess a superior electro-mechanical aptitude. He must understand the total operation and be able to think past the component, to how it interacts with others in the system. Above all, he must have the patience of a cat playing a mouse.

Regardless of a technician's competence, he can't render repairs to equipment without the proper implements. Before attempting to correct a problem, he must be armed with more than the pliers and screwdrivers he carries in his pouch. His knowledge, experience, gut instinct and a good set of troubleshooting guides are the tools he needs to get the job done.

THE PROCESS

Troubleshooting is the systematic analysis of a problem through a logical progression to determine its origin. Or to put it another way, it is the interpretation of the CAUSE and EFFECT relationship of faulty operation within a system or device.

The EFFECT is any condition, out of the ordinary, which exists as the result of a problem encountered within a system or device. It is invariably accompanied by one or more symptoms, giving rise to the problem. For instance, if a patient were laying unconscious on a table in an exam room and a physician, who had no prior knowledge of his condition, were brought in to diagnose his ailment, it's logical to assume that he would readily recognize the effect—the patient is out cold. In observing the patient, he recognizes certain symptoms that are evident. The patient may have a rapid heartbeat, be sweating profusely or what have you. By the use of deductive reasoning, the physician, without ever having to communicate with the patient, can conclude what CAUSED the problem to exhibit itself and take steps to correct it.

The analogy isn't unlike what might occur when a technician diagnoses the cause of a boiler shut down due to a high water condition. After a long weekend to cool off, the boiler may show zero pressure on its gauge, be sweating in the humid boiler room and its feed water pump might be pumping to beat the band. By reading the symptoms, he may determine that the feed water regulator failed and take action to correct the problem. In this case, the EFFECT was the shut down of the boiler and the CAUSE was the failure of an operating control.

The use of common sense, in concert with good diagnostic techniques and equipment, will enable the technician to diagnose the most difficult of problems.

TROUBLESHOOTING GUIDE

In the equipment repair war, the troubleshooters are your special forces. Before you send your troops on their first search and restore mission, you better arm them with these samplers to get them started. They will be creating their own guides before too long.

Figure 4-1. Troubleshooting Chart; Air Conditioning System

EFFECT	CAUSE	RECOMMENDATION
Discharge pressure too high	Fouled condenser	Clean tubes
	Non condensable gas in system	Purge unit
	Refrigerant overcharge	Purge unit
	Defective fan motor	Replace motor
	Location too hot	Provide adequate ventilation
Discharge pressure too low	Lack of refrigerant	Repair leak & recharge
	Leaky compressor discharge valves	Replace valves
	Condenser water too cold	Use alternate source
	Too much condenser water	Adjust regulating valve
	Location too cold	Relocate unit
Suction pressure too high	Expansion valve oversized	Replace valve
	Broken compressor suction valves	Replace valves
	Expansion valve stuck open	Clean or replace valve
	Refrigerant overcharge	Purge unit
	Evaporator fan malfunctioning	Correct
Suction pressure too low	Lack of refrigerant	Repair leak & recharge
	Obstructed metering device	Clean or replace device
	Expansion valve too small	Replace valve
	Liquid line strainer clogged	Clean strainer
	Evaporator not properly loaded	Clean evaporator
Space temperature too high	Lack of refrigerant	Repair leak & recharge
	Control setting too high	Reset control
	Restricted metering device	Repair or replace device
	Inadequate air circulation	Improve ventilation
	Unit undersized	Replace unit
Unit operates continuously	Excessive load	Check insulation
	Air infiltration	Close doors & windows
	Unit undercharged or overcharged	Correct charge
	Inefficient compressor	Replace compressor
	Air in system	Purge unit
Unit short cycles	Restricted metering device	Clean or replace device
	Supply water pressure too low	Correct
	Faulty motor	Replace motor
	Air in system	Purge unit
	Lack of refrigerant	Repair leak & recharge
Unit is noisy	Tubing vibrates	Secure tubing
	Worn fan motor bearings	Replace motor
	Dirty condenser	Clean condenser
	Fan blade hitting shroud	Repitch blades
	Compressor defective	Replace compressor
Unit will not run	Disconnect switch open	Make circuit
	Low voltage	Check incoming line
	Defective wiring	Replace wiring
	Relay inoperative	Clean contacts
	Blown fuse	Replace fuse

Figure 4-2. Troubleshooting Chart; Bearings

EFFECT	CAUSE	RECOMMENDATION
Extreme discoloration	Inadequate lubrication	Replace bearing
Wear	Loose fit on shaft	Replace bearing
	Dirt in the housing	Replace bearing
Corroded raceways	Use of wrong lubricant	Replace bearing
	Water in the housing	Replace bearing
Cracking and galling	Fatigue from age	Replace bearing
	Misalignment	Replace bearing
	Bearing loading too high	Replace bearing
Ceasing	Misalignment	Replace bearing
	Improperly mounted	Replace bearing
	Poor lubrication	Replace bearing
	Water in housing	Replace bearing

Figure 4-2. Troubleshooting Chart; Boiler Operation

EFFECT	CAUSE	RECOMMENDATION
Reduced Steam output	Fuel system failure	Check fuel trane components
	Malfunctioning pressure control	Recalibrate/replace control
Load imbalance between units	Flame failure	Check fuel trane components
Erratic water level	High solids concentrations	Increase blow down
	Malfunctioning water regulator	Perform slow drain test
Overpressure condition	Malfunctioning pressure control	Recalibrate/replace control
	Fuel valve stuck open	Repair valve
Smoking	Improper air supply	Check blower operation
	Poor fuel mixture	Check fuel-air ratio
High water level	Malfunctioning water regulator	Recalibrate/replace control
	Pump relay contacts frozen	Replace contacts or relay
		Drain boiler to normal level
Low water condition	Malfunctioning low water cut out	Repair or replace control
	Water supply valve closed	Open valve
	Feed water pump not energized	Check motor control panel
Carryover	High solids concentration	Increase blow down

Figure 4-4. Troubleshooting Chart; Burners

EFFECT	CAUSE	RECOMMENDATION
Fuel does not ignite	Defective transformer Improper electrode gap Pilot flame is out Improper air-fuel ratio	Check connections Reset gap Relight pilot Adjust fuel mixture
Flame is too large	Defective fuel regulator Burners overfiring	Replace regulator Reduce fuel input
Furnace side walls soot up	Flame impingement Orifice blocked or dirty	Adjust flame direction Clean opening
Burner rapid cycles	Programmer out of adjustment Defective pilot switch	Check cycle timer Replace switch
Flame out	Loss of fuel supply Programmer defective Loss of electrical power Flame detector failure	Check fuel trane components Repair or replace programmer Check feeder circuits Check signal amplifier

Figure 4-5. Troubleshooting Chart; Compressors

EFFECT	CAUSE	RECOMMENDATION
Failure to start	No power to motor Improperly wired Blown fuse, tripped breaker Overload tripped	Check motor control panel Check schematic & rewire Replace fuse, reset breaker Check motor for short
Less than rated delivery	Dirty inlet filter Worn piston rings System leaks Damaged valve parts	Clean or replace filter Replace rings Check piping & fittings Replace parts as needed
Erratic operation	Maladjusted control components Motor overloaded Piping restricted	Readjust components Check voltage to motor Clean out piping
High discharge temperature	Ambient temperature too high Improper lubrication Cylinder cooling fins clogged Discharge pressure too high	Improve room ventilation Check oil level Clean fins Adjust regulating control
Low operating pressure	Line leaks Worn piston rings Worn valve parts	Check and correct Replace rings Replace parts

Figure 4-6. Troubleshooting Chart; Cooling Towers

EFFECT	CAUSE	RECOMMENDATION
Excessive vibration	Fan out of alignment	Realign fan with motor
	Unbalanced fan	Repitch fan blades
	Loose v-belts	Check belts for tension
	Worn couplers	Replace couplers
	Worn shaft bearings	Replace bearings
	Bent shafts	Check shafts for trueness
	Loose connecting bolts	Tighten all connections
Unusual noises	Worn bearings	Replace bearings
	Motor single phased	Check electrical circuits
	Worn gear teeth	Adjust tooth engagement
	Motor fan hitting end bell	Replace fan
	Fan blade rubbing	Provide clearance for blades

Figure 4-7. Troubleshooting Chart; Electric Motors

EFFECT	CAUSE	RECOMMENDATION
Motor won't start	No power	Check electrical feed
	Low voltage	Compare nameplate to feed
	Load too great	Remove part of load
	Improper rotation	Reverse leads
	Open circuit in winding	Check for continuity
	Rotor defective	Replace rotor
	Driven unit locked	Check for obstructions
Motor runs at low speed	Control too far from motor	Relocate motor control
	Voltage too low at terminals	Check wire size
	Rotor bars broken	Replace rotor
	Incorrect brush tension	Check and correct
Motor noisy	Motor is single phased	Check incoming power
	Driven unit unbalanced	Correct
	Too much end play	Correct
	Poorly lubricated bearings	Check lubrication
	Rotor rubbing stator	Center rotor, replace bearings
	Loose coupler	Check alignment
	Loose motor mounting	Tighten holds down
Motor runs hot	Incorrect voltage	Compare nameplate to feed
	Housing is dirty	Clean all air passages
	Bent motor shaft	Straighten or replace
	Damaged bearings	Replace bearings
	Motor is single phased	Check incoming power

Figure 4-8. Troubleshooting Chart; Gas Fired Heaters & Incinerators

EFFECT	CAUSE	RECOMMENDATION
Pilot will not light	Dirty pilot orifice	Clean orifice
	Air in gas line	Bleed gas line
	Improper gas pressure	Adjust regulator
Unit puts out cold air	Defective fan control	Replace control
	Fan control improperly wired	Check schematics
Blower motor won't run	Blown fuse, tripped breaker	Replace fuse, reset breaker
	Open circuit	Check wiring
	Defective motor	Repair or replace
Motor running/ no pilot flame	Gas supply off	Open gas valves
	Ignition transformer faulty	Replace transformer

Figure 4-9. Troubleshooting Chart; Pumps

EFFECT	CAUSE	RECOMMENDATION
Less than rated delivery	Lack of priming	Fill suction end with liquid
	Leaky suction piping	Repair bad piping
	Impeller plugged	Dismantle and clean impeller
	Viscosity of liquid too high	Reduce viscosity by heating
	Air in the system	Bleed system
	Liquid too close to boiling	Lower temperature
	Worn valves and seats	Replace
Inadequate pressure	Air leaks in suction line	Repair lines, tighten flanges
	Low pump speed	Check motor
	Obstruction in pump	Dismantle and inspect
	Air in system	Bleed system

Chapter 5
PREVENTIVE MAINTENANCE

Even though we just extolled the need for a troubleshooting regimen in the plant, the fact is, if you have a workable preventive maintenance program in place, it will all but negate the troubleshooter position from the department's ranks. So you ask, "why not choose one or the other?" Because no matter how thorough your troubleshooter is or comprehensive your preventive maintenance program may be, your operation will eventually suffer if either is missing from the equipment care equation.

THE MECHANIC

To my mind, troubleshooting and preventive maintenance are inextricably linked. They can both provide proper, cost effective operation of plant equipment and extend its useful life. The procedures used in both processes are similar and the mechanical aptitude required of the technicians is markedly the same, precluding the need for separate personnel to fill both positions.

If your PM program is working for you, it should cut drastically into the need to troubleshoot your equipment, thereby freeing your troubleshooter to perform the PM function.

THE PROCESS

Preventive maintenance is the routine servicing of equipment on an established frequency aimed at extending its useful life and avoiding unnecessary down time.

The process involves the inspection, testing, lubrication, adjustment and cleaning of system components to detect early signs of deterioration and assure their continued operation. Benefits derived from a properly implemented program are improved operation, fewer failures, less down time, lower repair cost and longer equipment life.

There are a number of programs available that can be purchased off of the shelf, both manual and electronic, which will provide you with adequate guidance in caring for your equipment. I suggest that you assess your particular situation before espousing to a particular plan.

Whether you are planning on buying a canned PM program or constructing your own, you should ask yourself some questions before making a decision.

- Do I need to PM my entire inventory?
  Which items should be planned for?

- How much will it cost?
  For materials? For manpower?

- Are my mechanics qualified?
  What will it cost for training?

- How often should the PM be performed?
  Is it more cost effective to maintain or replace?

- Is my equipment under warranty?
  Should I extend the warranty or add the item to the program?

- Can I shut the units down for PM?
  How will it affect other operations?

- What seasonal equipment do I have?
  When do I shut it down?

- How will I document the results?
  Do I need to document everything?

- Would a service contract be less expensive?

Regardless of which direction you choose, your efforts will prove futile and costly unless you have an understanding of the tasks involved.

For your edification, I have compiled the following generic set of task sheets, listing minimal requirements for the major items typically found in a physical plant. These can be used as an aid in conceptualizing an in-house PM program. More specific information should be acquired from the manufacturers of the equipment in your individual plant and used when setting up your program.

PM TASK SHEETS

Figure 5-1. PM Task Sheet; Air Conditioning Systems

DAILY
Visually inspect
Check oil level
Record readings

MONTHLY
Remove and clean strainers
Check refrigerant level
Record amperages and voltages
Review operating logs
Check crankcase heater
Tighten loose connections
Observe purge operation
Check sight glasses

ANNUALLY
Clean and replace filters
Inspect bearings
Clean motors
Cleck electrical connections
Inspect heat exchange surfaces
Megger motor winding
Test relief valves
Troubleshoot the control circuit
Calibrate control cut in/out points
Tighten all loose connections

Figure 5-2. PM Task Sheet; Air Handling Units

DAILY
Check motor lubrication
Record temperatures, pressures, humidity
Inspect drive belts

MONTHLY
Inspect guards and pulleys
Check drive belt tension
Clean or replace filters
Clean and inspect coils
Check damper operation

ANNUALLY
Test coils for leaks
Check fan and housing integrity
Align V-belt drives
Inspect bearings
Check motor mounting
Calibrate controls
Megger motor windings
Record amperages and voltages
Clean condensate pan and drain
Clean plenums
Perform electrical safety check

Figure 5-3. PM Task Sheet; Boilers

DAILY
Observe operation
Blow down gauge glass
Test feed water regulator
Test low water fuel cut-off

MONTHLY
Test safety valve
Check burner linkage
Test flame failure control
Lubricate blower motor
Slow test low water fuel cut-off
Review water treatment logs

ANNUALLY
Dismantle and inspect appliances
Clean and inspect fireside
Clean and inspect waterside
Review operating logs
Dismantle and clean support equipment
Adjust flame
Revamp burner controls
Calibrate burner programmer
Replace indicator lamp bulbs
Operate all safety devices
Tighten loose connections
Inspect stack
Check chemical pump system
Inspect condensate return system

Figure 5-4. PM Task Sheet; Compressors

DAILY
Drain condensate
Check oil pressure and level
Observe operation
Check temperatures

MONTHLY
Calibrate gauges
Clean filters/strainers
Check pulley alignment
Check belt tension
Tighten hold downs
Operate safety devices
Clean unit
Clean air cooler fins

ANNUALLY
Change crankcase oil
Service air dryer unit
Review operator's log
Replace drive belts
Check tightness
Calibrate cut in/out pressure
Manually test safety valves
Change air filters
Check associated equipment
Replace bad piping sections
Overhaul per manufacturer's instruction

Figure 5-5. PM Task Sheet; Cooling Towers

DAILY
Check bearing temperatures
Check oil level
Check float valve operation
Lubricate as needed

MONTHLY
Review water treatment log
Clean debris from unit
Unclog all orifices
Check air inlet louvers
Check operation of make-up valve
Adjust bleed rate
Flush basins

ANNUALLY
Check fan blade pitch
Dismantle, clean and inspect unit
Inspect bearings and seals
Clean strainers
Check alignment of fan drive shaft
Brush tower slats
Check control switch operation
Record amperages and voltages
Inspect pulleys and replace belts

Figure 5-6. PM Task Sheet; Electric Motors

DAILY
Check lubrication level
Check bearing temperature
Observe operation

MONTHLY
Check motor mounting
Check belts and couplings
Inspect motor controller
Check conductor temperatures
Read amperages and voltages
Tighten loose connections

ANNUALLY
Megger windings
Clean and inspect
Check electrical connections
Inspect bearings and gears
Dry out housing
Overhaul per manufacturer's instructions

Figure 5-7. PM Task Sheet; Pumps

DAILY
Record pressures
Check oil level
Check packing leakage
Check bearing temperatures

MONTHLY
Check alignment
Inspect drive belts and pulleys
Check gauge calibration
Tighten mounting bolts
Check flexible couplers
Clean unit
Check piping for leaks

ANNUALLY
Inspect bearings
Replace packing
Check shaft for scoring
Check internally for weat
Clean and inspect strainers
Change crankcase oil
Overhaul per manufacturer's instruc-
 tions

Chapter 6
WATER TREATMENT

Thanks for the offer but I'm all coffeed out. I truly believe if ever my kidneys were opened they would find coffee beans in place of stones. How about some water instead? There's nothing more refreshing than a cold glass of water in a hot machinery room. But did you know that the tap water we can't live without could prove fatal to your equipment? The substances commonly found in water have the potential to corrode metal, choke fluid passages and allow vessels to overheat to the point of failure. Interesting stuff you say? Let me tell you more about it.

Water is at once our most precious and abundant natural resource. Needless to say, life ceases to exist without it and is adversely affected when reserves are low. Hundreds of billions of gallons a day are used to irrigate farming fields. Billions more are distributed each day for drinking, bathing, cooking, and washing cars. Other hundreds of billions of gallons are used each day by industry. Where does it come from? Where does it go after it's been used? Will it all be gone some day?

THE WATER CYCLE

The oceans are natural reservoirs and the primary source of all water consumed on our planet. Their waters are heated by the sun causing them to vaporize. The water vapor created by this action is passed skyward through a process of natural circulation, eventually forming clouds. When brought into contact with cold air in the upper atmosphere, the clouds discharge their moisture in the form of rain, snow and ice which falls to the earth's surface due to its gravitational pull. Much of the water re-evaporates into the atmosphere but most is left behind to find its way back to the oceans by natural flow, sometimes first passing through the pipelines of man.

Water, as a vapor, is colorless, tasteless, and odorless. It is H_2O in its purest form; two parts of hydrogen to one part of oxygen. It's when it falls from the sky that it begins to take on the characteristics that cause us all the headaches down here. And it gets much worse before it arrives at our taps.

COMMON IMPURITIES

As rain is hurled earthward, it absorbs dissolved oxygen and carbon dioxide in the air, making it corrosive. Other impurities in the air attach themselves to the droplets turning the rainwater into an acidic slurry. When it comes into contact with the ground it picks up impurities through the erosion process as it passes over the land seeking a lower level. Ground waters, such as springs and wells, pick up minerals as the water seeps through the rock strata. Surface waters, such as lakes, streams and rivers contain silt and organic materials as well as the pollutants of man. The types of impurities found in water supplies vary with the source.

Figure 6-1 lists the more common impurities which can affect operations in the physical plant. As can be seen in the table, they cause scale formation, corrosion and fouling of system components; each of which can lay waste to your equipment.

Figure 6-1. Common Water Impurities

IMPURITY	SOURCE	EFFECT
Algae	Organic Growth	Fouling
Calcium	Mineral Deposits	Scale/Corrosion
Carbon Dioxide	Dissolved Gasses	Corrosion
Chloride	Mineral Deposits	Corrosion
Free Acids	Industrial Wastes	Corrosion
Hardness	Mineral Deposits	Scale
Magnesium	Mineral Deposits	Scale
Oxygen	Dissolved Gasses	Corrosion
Silica	Mineral Deposits	Scale
Suspended Solids	Undissolved Matter	Fouling/Scale

SCALE is a very hard substance which is created when mineral salts come out of solution as their solubility decreases with an increase in the temperature of the water. The scale-forming salts tend to adhere directly to heating surfaces forming layer after layer of insulation on the metal, thereby decreasing its heat transfer efficiency. Scale results in metal fatigue and failure due to overheating, energy waste, higher maintenance costs and unnecessary safety risks. A one-sixteenth-inch thickness in a fire tube boiler can cause an eleven percent increase in fuel consumption. Any accumulation can cause problems.

CORROSION is the attacking of metals by acids or electrolytic action. The metal is eaten away in a fashion such as the general wasting of an automobile fender or by localized pitting. Corrosion increases downtime and maintenance costs, results in premature replacement of equipment and causes unnecessary safety risks.

FOULING is a condition whereby restrictions develop in piping and equipment passages resulting in less than efficient flow. Although these accumulations are undesirable, they don't usually pose the same dangers as scale or corrosion and can be easily corrected. The major consequences of fouling are energy waste and increased operating and maintenance costs.

Aside from the three common problems already mentioned, poor quality water can also result in foaming, priming and embrittlement. Foaming is a condition where frothy bubbles, resembling the head on a beer are created in the steam space of a boiler by concentrations of soluble sodium salts aggravated by oil, grease, suspended solids or organic matter. Priming is a consequence of foaming whereby the frothy bubbles break and the resulting liquid combines to form slugs or water which are carried over into its steam system. Embrittlement is a condition whereby small, hairline cracks appear in highly stressed areas due to high concentrations of alkaline salts that liberate hydrogen which is absorbed by the iron in the steel which changes its physical properties.

Scale formation, corrosion and equipment fouling need not be a major concern in the physical plant. With the implementation of a well monitored water treatment program, these and their associated problems can be all but avoided.

VENDOR SERVICES

I know you're not a chemical engineer and yes you can't be expected to know everything about everything and . . . This is one area where you may need, and for that matter be entitled to, assist-

ance from the outside. The investment you make in a service agreement with a reputable chemical vendor may well pay dividends in
short order when you consider the potential for loss you have without one. But before thumbing through the yellow pages for the
nearest company, you should first ask yourself some questions.

- Where do I need water treatment?
  The boilers? The chillers? Equipment water jackets?

- What's the condition of the water locally?
  Do I need a softener?

- How much is budgeted for water treatment?
  Can I justify a payback?

- What services will I need?
  Can I do some testing in-house?

- Which company should I use?
  Can I get competitive bids?

A preferred method for quelling many of your concerns is to
contact your peers in comparably sized facilities and ask for their
input. They can fill you in on the problems and successes they have
experienced in their own operations. My contribution is this thought;
chemicals are chemicals and a water treatment company is only as
good as the representative they assign to service your account.

SERVICE AGREEMENTS

Whichever company you choose to analyze your waters and supply you with chemicals, make certain that your agreement with them
is in black and white and signed by an appropriate officer of their
firm.

The agreement should stipulate exactly what the salesperson had
agreed to verbally. It should state the number and frequency of visits
to expect from the representative and the work he will perform during those visits. It should address call backs for emergencies, tell you
what training will be provided for your people and spell out the
technical assistance available for problems you may encounter.

Everything in this world is negotiable. Never let a salesperson talk
you into signing an agreement that was written by and in the best
interests of the company you are attempting to contract with.

VENDOR RESPONSIBILITIES

At a minimum, the vendor should:

- Become familiar with your equipment and its frequency of operation
- Survey all of your water systems and supply you with a written proposal indicating your problem areas and what can be done to correct them
- Provide you with a written analysis of your waters, indicating what constituents were found and in what amounts, on an agreed upon frequency
- Recommend treatments and proper feeding methods for each system
- Train your personnel to test your waters in-house and provide log sheets for recording the results
- Establish parameters to guide your operators in the use of chemicals and methods for their introduction into and removal from your equipment.
- Make feed and bleed/blowdown recommendations
- Apprise you of D.E.R. and E.P.A. restrictions
- Interpret the results of your in-house tests and make recommendations to improve your operation
- Perform internal inspections on your equipment
- Establish a chemical inventory and determine reorder levels
- Provide laboratory support such as metalurgical and microbiological analysis
- Modify your program to meet federal, state and local regulatory requirements

YOUR COMMITMENT

A water treatment program cannot succeed without the commitment of both the vendor and the owner in assuring its success. If the vendor only wants to sell you chemicals, you should toss him out into the parking lot and if you aren't prepared to do your part, you might as well join him.

Higher fuel costs, increased safety risks, unnecessary equipment replacements and overtime premiums are consequences of a poorly devised and ill managed water treatment program. The vendor's representative can follow the service agreement to the letter but it's up to you to provide the direction needed to meet the demands of your operation.

Chapter 7
POWER PLANT OPERATIONS

Quit complaining, I'm just as hot and tired as you are. How do you think the operator feels about being down here on a full-time basis? I'll just touch on a few more equipment concerns, then we can leave the machinery spaces for the relative comfort of your office.

CERTIFICATES AND PERMITS

Depending on where you are located, the operation of certain items in your inventory may fall under the auspices of some jurisdictional authority. In Pennsylvania, for example, the Department of Labor and Industry requires that certain boilers undergo semiannual inspection and pressure vessels, biannual inspections by an authorized inspector who reports his findings to the State for evaluation. If the findings are acceptable per the inspector's recommendations, the State issues a certificate of operation (Figure 7-1) which upon receipt by the owner, must be posted in a conspicuous place, near the equipment. Operation of jurisdictional equipment without a certificate can result in legal penalties for the owner and operator.

Certain elevators are required to be inspected quarterly and their certificates of operation (Figure 7-2) must be posted in the area. Due to problems of vandalism and petty thievery, it's a good idea to post copies of the certificates where prescribed and to keep the originals under lock and key in the office files.

Permits may also be required from other entities such as the Department of Environmental Resources which issues permits for incinerator operation (Figure 7-3) and sewage (Figure 7-4).

Electrical inspections must be performed on all new installations and certified (Figure 7-5) as safe and conforming with the National Electrical Code and local ordinances.

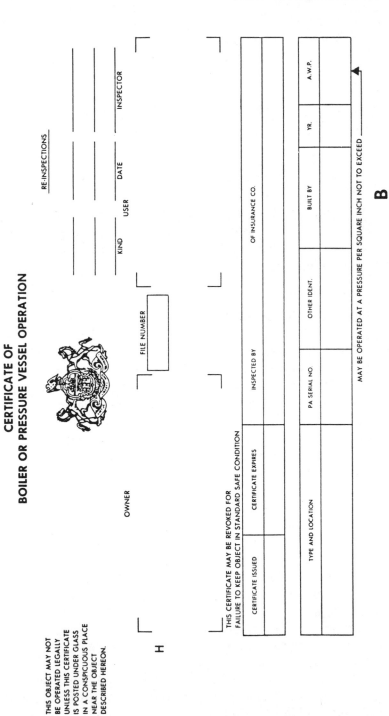

Figure 7-1. Boiler/Pressure Vessel Operating Certificate

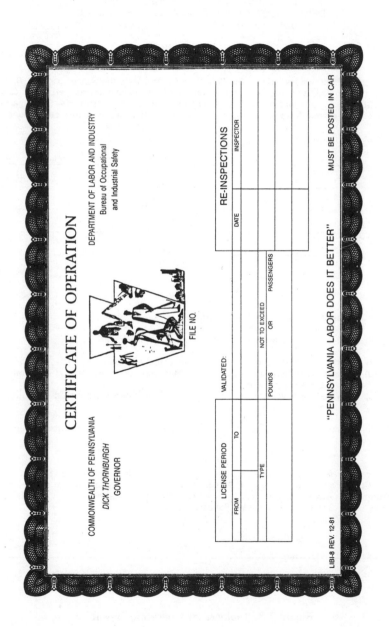

Figure 7-2. Elevator Operating Certificate

ER–AQ–28
Rev: 6/79

COMMONWEALTH OF PENNSYLVANIA
DEPARTMENT OF ENVIRONMENTAL RESOURCES
BUREAU OF AIR QUALITY CONTROL

OPERATING PERMIT

In accordance with provisions of the Air Pollution Control Act, the Act of January 8, 1960, P.L. 2119, as amended, and after due consideration of an application received under Chapter 127 of the rules and regulations of the Department of Environmental Resources, the Department hereby issues this permit for the operation of the air contamination source described below.

Permit No. _____   Source & _____

Owner   _____   Air   _____

Address   _____   Cleaning _____

           _____   Device   _____

Attention: _____   Location _____

           _____   _____

This permit is subject to the following conditions:

    (1) That the source and any associated air cleaning devices are to be:

        (a) operated in such a manner as not to cause air pollution;
        (b) in compliance with the specifications and conditions of the plan approval issued under the same number;
        (c) operated and maintained in a manner consistent with good operating and maintenance practices.

    (2) This permit is valid only for the specific equipment, location and owner named above.

Failure to comply with the conditions placed on this permit is a violation of Section 127.25. Violation of this or any other provision of Article III of the rules and regulations of the Department of Environmental Resources will result in suspension or revocation of this permit and/or prosecution under Section 9 of the Air Pollution Control Act.

Issued _____   _____

Expires _____   Regional Air Pollution Control Engineer

Figure 7-3. Incinerator Operating Permit

ER—BWQ—291: Rev. 4-84
(Formerly ER—BCE—129)

*SEE REVERSE SIDE FOR IMPORTANT INFORMATION

PERMIT
for
INSTALLATION OF SEWAGE DISPOSAL SYSTEM

Pursuant to Application for Sewage Disposal System number _____
a permit is hereby issued to:

NAME OF APPLICANT

ADDRESS OF APPLICANT   TELEPHONE NUMBER

PROPERTY ADDRESS OF SITE FOR SEWAGE DISPOSAL SYSTEM

This Permit issued under the provisions of the "Pennsylvania Sewage Facilities Act", the Act of January 24, 1966 (P.L. 1535), as amended is subject to the following conditions:

1. Except as otherwise provided by the Act or regulations of the Pennsylvania Department of Environmental Resources, no part of the installation shall be covered until inspected by the approving body and approval to cover is granted in writing below.

2. This Permit may be revoked for the reasons set forth in Section 7(b)(6) of the Act.

3. If construction or installation of an individual sewage system or community sewage system and of any building or structure for which such system is to be installed has not commenced within two years after the issuance of a permit for such system, the said permit shall expire, and a new permit shall be obtained prior to the commencement of said construction or installation.

ADDITIONAL CONDITIONS:

KEEP THIS PERMIT FOR FUTURE REFERENCE

Approval to Cover   Date of Issuance of Permit _____

_____   _____
Signature of Enforcement Officer   Approving Body

_____   _____
Date   Signature of Enforcement Officer

The basis for the issuance of this Permit is the information supplied in the Application for Sewage Disposal System and other pertinent data concerning soil absorption tests, topography, lot size, and sub-soil groundwater table elevations. The permit only indicates that the issuing authority is satisfied that the installation of the Sewage Disposal System is in accordance with the Rules, Regulations and Standards adopted by the Pennsylvania Department of Environmental Resources under the provisions of the Pennsylvania Sewage Facilities Act, the Act of January 24, 1966 (P.L. 1535), as amended. The issuance of a Permit shall not preclude the enforcement of other health laws, ordinances or regulations in the case of malfunctioning of the system.

TO BE POSTED AT THE BUILDING SITE

FORM PROVIDED BY THE PENNSYLVANIA DEPARTMENT OF ENVIRONMENTAL RESOURCES

Figure 7-4. Sewage Systems Permit

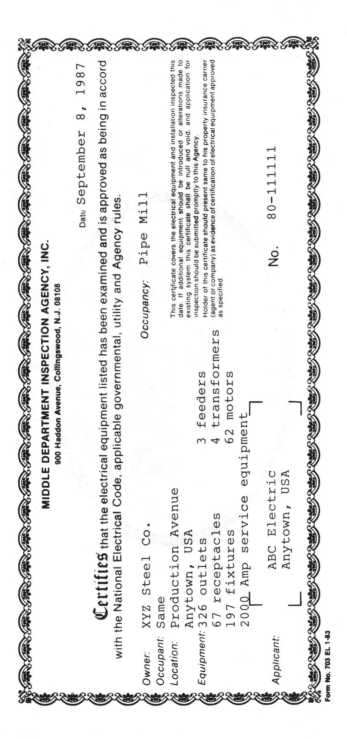

Figure 7-5. Electrical Inspection Certificate

OPERATORS' LICENSES

Not all municipalities require that equipment operators be licensed. Some governing bodies sanction licensing of operators throughout their jurisdiction. Often only the larger cities in some states have a licensure requirement.

This lack of standardization is a source of frustration for managers who must rely on the expertise of the personnel charged with the responsibility of equipment operation in their buildings.

Over the years state legislators have been petitioned by many groups concerned with the safe operation of power plant equipment to enact laws which would require equipment operators to prove their competence by examination prior to being given permission to operate boilers, pressure vessels and high energy mechanical devices within their jurisdictions. Lobbyists of many ilks have succeeded in persuading them that the laws were not necessary and subsequently the legislation was dropped.

As our society progresses technically, our systems become more complex, our controls more sophisticated and our operators are left in the dark. Training alone will not remedy the situation. An operator needs to bring certain skills to the job as a base to build on; his credentials, if you will.

Even if there are no governmental requirements for licensing of operators in your metropolitan area, it would behoove you to hire operators licensed or certified by some regulatory or academic body. Though the licensing or certification may not proclaim him an expert in his field, it is at least proof that he has demonstrated sufficient knowledge of the subject on which he was tested to a higher authority.

When licensed operators are not readily available, you should establish an environmental conducive to the acquisition of licenses or certificates of competency by your personnel. This can be accomplished through a regimen of in-house instruction, on-the-job training, seminar attendance and formal schooling.

A well implemented program leading to professional designations for your employees will promote improved morale and instill a professional attitude within the department. The dividends of increased productivity and decreased expenses will far surpass any financial outlay for the program.

In the City of Pittsburgh, operators are required by statute (Figure 7-6) to make application (Figure 7-7) for license (Figure 7-8) to operate boilers and other pressure vessels. They must be sponsored by licensed operators and/or employers, undergo proctored testing and are assessed fees for examinations and licensure.

With the exception of boilers and engines under the jurisdiction of the United States and locomotive boilers and engines, the State of Ohio requires that "any person who desires to operate or have charge of a stationary steam boiler of more than thirty horsepower, except boilers which are in the charge of a licensed engineer, must make application (Figures 7-9 A & B) to the district examiner of steam engineers upon a blank furnished by the examiner and shall pass an examination on the construction and operation of steam boilers, steam pumps and hydraulics, under such rules and regulations as may be adopted by the chief examiner of steam engineers, which rules and regulations and standard of examination shall be uniform throughout the state."

Appendix A lists the State of Ohio license laws and rules governing the examination of applicants for licenses as stationary steam engineers and boiler operators. Although Ohio does not set the rules for the rest of the country, their license laws are typical of the regulations you will find in the jurisdictions where such laws have been enacted and can serve as a guide to the licensure of operators everywhere.

Courses of instruction leading to certification of operators' skills are available from local colleges, technical schools, engineering societies and professional associations such as BOMA (The Building Owners and Managers Association International). For example, BOMA, through its educational arm, BOMI (The Building Owners and Managers Institute International) offers courses of instruction and examinations culminating in certification.

The Systems Maintenance Technician (SMT) certificate (Figure 7-10) is earned after successful completion of studies in the areas of heating systems, refrigeration, air handling, electrical systems and controls.

By adding courses on building design and maintenance, energy management and supervision, the S.M.T. can acquire the Systems Maintenance Administrator (S.M.A.) designation (Figure 7-11).

Whichever way you approach it, there is no substitute for knowledge. Your operators will appreciate the interest you will have taken in the furtherance of their education and the designations will project an image of professionalism within your department.

CHAPTER 745 - STATIONARY ENGINEERS

745.01 License required and Exceptions   745.04 Only Licensess to operate equipment
745.02 Written Examination   745.05 Suspension or revocation
745.03 Qualifications of Applicant   745.06 License Fee

745.01 LICENSE REQUIRED; EXCEPTIONS

No person shall control or operate pipes, boilers, stationary or locomotive engines, or any other containers, tanks or vessels under pressure of water, liquid, gas or steam without first obtaining a license from the License Office- However, the following are excepted from licensing requirements;

(a) Pipes, containers or vessels used in the transportation of water, liquid, gas or steam;
(b) Hot water tanks used for domestic service as defined in the Mechanical Code;
(c) Portable compressor operators; and
(d) All vessels defined as low pressure in the Mechanical Code or any vessel of fifteen (15) pounds per square inch or less of pressure.

745.02 WRITTEN EXAMINATION

(a) A written examination shall be given by the License Officer to insure all applicants comprehend the operation of pressure vessels for the safety of life and property, and a license shall only be issued to the applicant who receives a passing grade. Examinations and licenses may be issued under different classifications as determined by the License Officer.
(b) The fee for such examination shall be twenty-five ($25.00) dollars, which, if passed, shall be credited to the license fee.

745.03 QUALIFICATIONS OF APPLICANT

In addition to the qualifications enumerated in Section 701.04 for all applicants for licenses, an applicant for a stationary engineer license, or any classification thereof, shall:
(a) Be eighteen (18) years of age and able to read and speak the English language;
(b) Possess two (2) years practical experience as evidenced by a certification thereof by a licensed stationary engineer; and
(c) Pass a test in accordance with Section 745.02.

745.04 ONLY LICENSEES TO OPERATE EQUIPMENT

No owner, lessee or agent thereof, of any pipes, containers, boilers, stationary or locomotive engines, tanks or other vessels within the scope of this chapter, or any person acting for such owner, lessee or agent shall permit any unlicensed person to operate or control such equipment. No unlicensed person shall operate or control such equipment. The licensed person in charge of or operating the aforesaid equipment must be located on the same premises where said equipment is located during such operation or control.

745.05 SUSPENSION OR REVOCATION

The License Officer, upon investigation shall suspend the license of any licensee who is incompetent, has been guilty of negligence, has endangered life or property or willfully violated any provision of this chapter. Revocation shall be as required in Section 701.14(b).

745.06 LICENSE FEE

The fee for an initial stationary engineer license shall be fifty ($50.00) dollars per year and the fee for a renewal thereof shall be twenty-five ($25.00) dollars if renewed within thirty (30) days of expiration, otherwise the initial fee shall be paid without re-examination.
* * * * * * * * * *

Please bring on day of test: Test will be given on the second Wednesday of:

    Check or Money Order (No Cash)   January   July
    Completed Application, including   March   September
    Pen   Notary   May   November

TEST IS OPEN BOOK   TEST TIME: 1:00 p.m.

Figure 7-6. Stationary Engineers Licensure Statute

★ PLEASE READ BOTH SIDES OF THIS APPLICATION CAREFULLY ★

CITY OF PITTSBURGH

BUILDING INSPECTION   **LICENSE NO.** _____

APPLICATION FOR LICENSE TO OPERATE BOILERS AND OTHER PRESSURE VESSELS
★ ★

NAME _____   PHONE NO. (____) _____

ADDRESS _____
                                          (CITY)   (STATE)   (ZIP)

APPLICATION FOR: ☐ STEAM BOILER FIREMAN   ☐ STATIONARY ENGINEER

Are you eighteen (18) years of age or over and able to read and speak English? ☐YES ☐NO

Do you possess two (2) years pratical experience as evidenced below? ☐ YES ☐ NO

PRESENT EMPLOYER: _____   NO. OF YEARS? _____

EMPLOYER'S ADDRESS: _____
                                          (CITY)   (STATE)   (ZIP)
POSITION OR DUTIES: _____

If less than two (2) years,
PREVIOUS EMPLOYER: _____   NO. OF YEARS? _____

PREVIOUS EMPLOYER'S ADDRESS: _____
                                          (CITY)   (STATE)   (ZIP)
POSITION OR DUTIES: _____

Two (2) of the following four (4) signatures are required. Copy of military records
  indicating experience is acceptable as one of the signatures.

"We the undersigned certify that the above named applicant has the experience required by law
and is qualified to perform the duties for which application for license is made."

1. _____   3. _____
   Licensed Operator   Reg. No.   Licensed Operator   Reg. No.

2. _____   4. _____
   Present Employer   Previous Employer
★ ★

STATE OF PENNSYLVANIA)
                     (SS
COUNTY OF ALLEGHENY)
The applicant, being duly sworn, deposes and says that all information given in this applica-
tion is true and correct.
Sworn to and subscribed before me this _____ day
of _____ 19 ____.   _____
                                                  Signature of Applicant

_____
Notary Public
★ ★

DATE OF EXAMINATION ___/___/___, SCORE_____, ACTION_____, BY_____
                                                                   Examiner
EXAMINATION FEE: $ _25_.00   LICENSE FEE: $ _25_.00
VALIDATION: VALIDATION:
              ★ ALL LICENSES EXPIRE ON MARCH 31 ★
                                                        (over)

Figure 7-7. Application for Stationary Engineers License

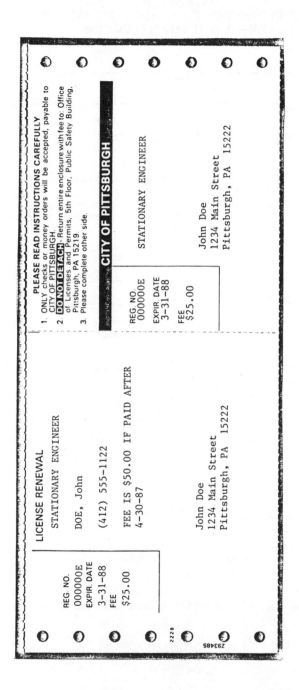

Figure 7-8. Stationary Engineers License

STATE OF OHIO
DEPARTMENT OF INDUSTRIAL RELATIONS
EXAMINERS OF STEAM ENGINEERS

I _____
(Name)

_____
(Address)   (City)   (State)   (Zip)

_____
(Area Code)   (Telephone Number)

Request permission to sit for ( ) steam engineer, ( ) high pressure boiler operator, ( ) low pressure boiler operator examination to obtain a license.

This request must be received by the Examiner at least fourteen (14) days prior to the date you can be assigned. If your request is approved, you will be assigned an examination date within sixty (60) days of date request was received.

Date requested to sit for examination

1st Preference _____

2nd Preference _____

If you are using schooling in steam boiler operation, boiler maintenance, or steam engineering, power plant maintenance as credit for part of your experience, complete the form below or preferably attach a copy of your **Certificate of Course Completion.**

Number of hours attended _____

_____
Instructor's Name and Certificate Number

Name of School _____

Address of School _____

_____

Telephone Number _____
(Area Code)

_____
Signature of Instructor or Director of School

PLEASE COMPLETE THE FORM ON REVERSE SIDE.

Figure 7-9a. Equipment Operators License Application

STATE OF OHIO
DEPARTMENT OF INDUSTRIAL RELATIONS
EXAMINERS OF STEAM ENGINEERS

CERTIFICATION OF EXPERIENCE

This form is to be signed by persons who have knowledge of your experience; preferably, one of whom is in possession of a Stationary Steam Engineer's or Boiler Operator's License.

I certify _____ has
(Applicant's Name)
had _____ hours practical experience as a ( ) steam engineer, ( ) oiler, ( ) boiler operator, ( ) boiler operator's helper, or ( ) boiler repair person, experienced with duties that pertain to ( ) steam engine, ( ) steam turbine, or ( ) steam boiler operation; and has had _____ hours ( ) maintenance, ( ) construction on steam engines, steam turbines, or steam boilers; the experience was

acquired at _____
(Name of Company or Firm)   (Address)

Signed _____
(SIGNATURE MUST BE NOTARIZED)

Title _____

Address _____

Date _____   Phone Number _____
(Area Code)

★ ★ ★ ★ ★ ★ ★

I certify _____ has
had _____ hours practical experience as a ( ) steam engineer, ( ) oiler, ( ) boiler operator, ( ) boiler operator's helper, or ( ) boiler repair person, experienced with duties that pertain to ( ) steam engine, ( ) steam turbine, or ( ) steam boiler operation; and has had _____ hours ( ) maintenance, ( ) construction on steam engines, steam turbines, or steam boilers; the experience was

acquired at _____
(Name of Company or Firm)   (Address)

Signed _____
(SIGNATURE MUST BE NOTARIZED)

Title _____

Address _____

Date _____   Phone Number _____
(Area Code)

In lieu of this form, a DD214 will be accepted with proper classification and service time.

Experience must be acquired on equipment with a manufacturer's rating of at least thirty (30) horse power.

DIR 1503   Form 430

Figure 7-9b. Certification of Experience

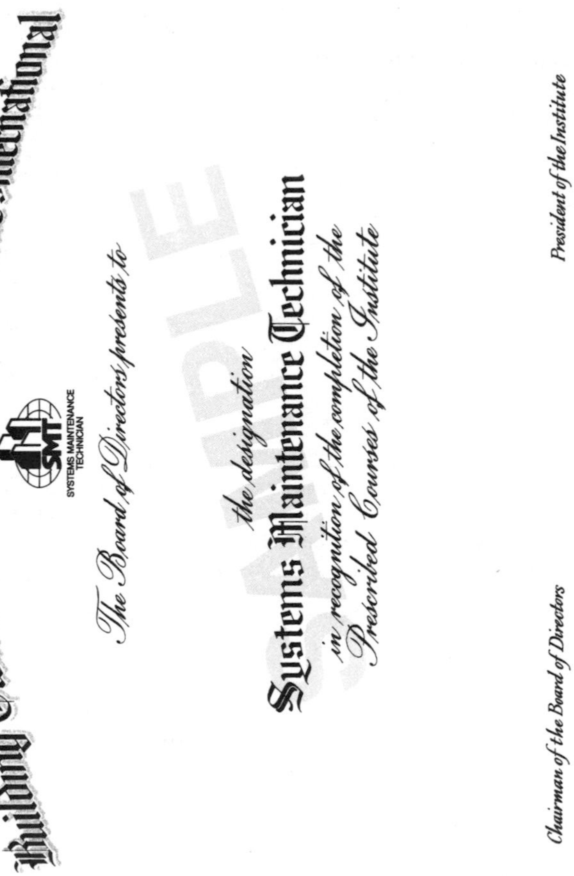
Building Owners and Managers Institute International

SMT
SYSTEMS MAINTENANCE TECHNICIAN

The Board of Directors presents to

the designation

Systems Maintenance Technician

in recognition of the completion of the
Prescribed Courses of the Institute

SAMPLE

Chairman of the Board of Directors

President of the Institute

Figure 7-10. Certificate; Systems Maintenance Technician. (Courtesy: Building Owners and Managers Institute.)

Figure 7-11. Certificate; Systems Maintenance Administrator. (Courtesy: Building Owners and Managers Institute.)

OPERATING INSTRUCTIONS

Due to employee attrition, constant operation of equipment for long periods and the lack of familiarization with the operation of devices by operators transferred from other areas, you should post a complete set of operating instructions for each device, by each device.

They should state, step-by-step, how to start up, operate and shut down the device. They should also detail what action to take during emergencies and indicate normal operating pressure and temperature ranges. Some plant engineers make it a habit to mark the ranges on the gauges or thermometers themselves to provide a visual indication of the operation, at a glance.

The instructions should be typewritten and mounted in a transparent jacket that is impervious to the elements it is exposed to such as steam, oil, water and soot.

EQUIPMENT ROUNDS

A power plant routine should be written and strictly adhered to. It should trace the direction the operator is to take in witnessing the operation of the systems in his charge, and specify his duties for inspecting and testing their components. It should indicate what readings are to be taken, what documents to record and the reporting process he must use in relaying his findings to the plant manager's office. The routine may include responsibility for water testing and treatment, lubrication, alternating the operation of system components, housekeeping duties and security rounds.

OPERATING LOGS

The information recorded in operating logs serves many purposes. It informs operators of existing conditions when taking over a shift and of occurrences experienced during prior shifts. It provides a chronological history of equipment operation and down times and red flags nuisance problems. It serves as the eyes and ears of the plant manager in his absence and provides actuarial data for determining equipment repair and replacement needs. In a court of law, it can be considered a legal document for purposes of litigation.

The formats used for recording information concerning the operation of power plants are as numerous as the plants in which they are found. Some logs are simple checklists indicating which devices are operating, others require only temperatures and pressures to be recorded, while still others call for elaborate narratives to be written on each piece of equipment. However you choose to construct yours, make certain that they are filled in completely, submitted to you in a timely fashion and appropriately filed for later reference.

EQUIPMENT FAILURE

Nothing simply fails without cause. Though the reason for failure of a device may not be readily apparent, it makes sense to investigate the incident to prevent a recurrence. All that is needed to assure future successes is a thorough understanding of past failures.

Much can be learned by reviewing the logs and interviewing the operator. What happened? When did it happen? What conditions existed prior to the occurrence? What was damaged? How long was it down? Who was affected? What was done to correct the problem? Where are the bad parts?

Avoid premature conclusions. Once your questions have been answered, have the failed parts sent out to an independent laboratory for analysis. Armed with the results, determine if the accident resulted from mechanical failure or human error, then take measures to correct the problem.

Chapter 8
MANAGEMENT AIDS

As long as we're back in the office, let's discuss what support items you should find here to help you in your work and how they affect and are affected by your operation. The best place to start is with the operations bible, the S.O.P. manual.

THE STANDARD
OPERATING PROCEDURES MANUAL

Without rules and guidelines, organizations are doomed to failure from their inception. To assure their continuity, religions have their holy books, athletic teams, their play books and we have our S.O.P. manuals.

If properly assembled and maintained, an S.O.P. manual will mirror your department and address every facet of its operation. It should stipulate department policy governing employee dress, equipment acquisition and contingency planning; contain valve, switch and equipment master lists; spell out procedures for rounds routines, snow removal and equipment operation and cover aspects of safety, housekeeping, and documentation. In short, everything involved in or involving the operation of your department should be referenced in the manual.

Although I prescribe no set format for creating the instrument, I suggest you thoroughly think through its construction before attempting to establish yours.

Figure 8-1 is a condensed table of contents for an S.O.P. manual of a small physical plant. The area headed SECTION divides the manual, reflecting different aspects of the operation. The SUBSECTION area lists policies, procedures and various other data related to each section. The OPP policies and procedures are those established by the parent organization to which all departments must conform. The PO policies and procedures are those written by and for the department. The MNT policies and procedures deal directly with the maintenance section of the physical plant department.

The ORGANIZATIONAL section states the scope, function and objectives of the department; lists the parent organization's policy on departmental policies and procedures; includes organizational charts of the department and parent organization; establishes the maintenance section within the department and provides an explanation of the management style used by the corporation.

The FINANCIAL section lists the corporation's policies on monetary expenditures and vendors used by the department; contains the department's man-hour, operating and capital budgets and includes the contracts issued for the physical plant.

The PERSONNEL section contains the corporate policies governing all aspects of employment within its ranks, the department's employee policies, guides for orientation and training, job descriptions and a written safety presentation given by the physical plant director to all new employees in the corporation.

The OPERATIONAL section addresses working hours, dress codes, specific duties of the maintenance section, inclement weather routines and water analyses; contains an index of all drawings used in the facility and provides copies of all the schedules, logs and forms used by the department.

The EQUIPMENT section provides an index of all operating manuals, sites maintenance procedures and sets the parameters for equipment testing and operation.

The PREVENTIVE MAINTENANCE section explains the department's PM program, contains copies of rounds routines and provides guidelines for ancillary equipment care.

The SAFETY section explains the corporate safety program, supplies a list of general safety rules, establishes the duties of the safety director and provides general and electrical safety standards.

The FIRE section addresses all facets of fire safety, smoking policies, testing and inspection of fire equipment and systems, corporate policies on fire drills and the storage of combustibles.

The EMERGENCY section contains procedures for providing essential services during extraordinary circumstances, evacuation of personnel during emergency situations and a telephone list for call-in capability of in-house personnel and outside services.

Figure 8-1. S.O.P. Manual; Table of Contents

SECTION	SUB-SECTION

Organizational	— Scope/function
	— Objectives
	— Organizational Charts
	— Management by Objectives Guidelines
	— Department policy/procedure list
	— Policies
	  * OPP 2.2 Organizational policies
	  * MNT 1.0 Maintenance section organization
	  * MNT 1.1 Maintenance section standards

Financial	— Policies
	  * OPP 1.44 Capitalization
	  * OPP 1.48 Purchase order
	  * OPP 1.50 Blanket purchase order
	  * OPP 1.46 Equipment acquisition
	  * PO-013 Contracts manual
	— Vendor list
	— Department Budgets

Personnel	— Policies
	  * PO-002 Employee orientation
	  * OPP 1.23 Orientation program
	  * OPP 2.30 Job description
	  * OPP 2.40 Seminar and workshop
	  * OPP 2.7 Seminar attendance
	  * OPP 2.8 Inservice attendance
	  * MNT 1.4 Maintenance dept. training
	— Job Descriptions
	— Safety Presentation

Operational	— Policies
	  * MNT 2.0 Duties of maintenance dept.
	  * PO-003 Department work hours
	  * PO-004 Work requisition system
	  * MNT 2.5 Extreme weather preparation
	  * MNT 3.0 Work dress uniform
	— Procedures
	  * PO-005 Winter groundskeeping
	  * PO-010 Shop/job cleanup
	  * PO-001 Maintenance cart rounds routine
	  * MNT 1.3 Maintenance department security
	  * PO-017 Water treatment program
	— Schedules
	— Forms
	— Drawing Index

Figure 8-1 *(Continued)*

SECTION	SUB-SECTION

Equipment
— Policies
  * PO-006   Emergency generator testing schedule
  * MNT 2.4   Freeze protection
— Procedures
  * PO-007   Emergency generator testing
  * PO-008   Operating instructions — generator
  * MNT 2.27 Cleaning of incinerator

Preventive Maintenance
— Policies
  * PO-011   Preventive maintenance program
-- Procedures
  * MNT 2.25 Humidity control guidelines
  * PO-011.1   Preventive maintenance rounds
  * PO-011.2   Mechanical rounds routine
  * MNT 2.22 Lawn equipment
  * PO-011.3   Preventive maintenance — generator
  * MNT 2.20 Dietary equipment
  * MNT 2.21 Vehicles

Safety
— Policies
  * OPP 1.17 General safety rules
  * OPP 1.24 Safety program
  * OPP 2.21 Risk management/safety committee
  * PO-014   Department safety
— General Procedures
  * OPP 2.37 Safety inspection
  * OPP 2.51 Hot water temperatures
— Electrical Procedures
  * OPP 1.26   Electrical safety program
  * OPP 2.60 Use of personal electrical appliances
  * OPP 2.47 Extension cords/adapters
  * PO-016   Department electrical safety

Fire
— Policies
  * MNT 2.6   Maintenance of automatic sprinkler system
  * OPP 1.25 Fire drill
  * MNT 2.7   Fire extinguisher inspection/testing
  * OPP 1.4   Smoking
  * MNT 2.19 Fire warning system
  * OPP 2.35 Use/storage of flammable liquids
— Procedures
  * OPP 1.34 Fire procedure

Figure 8-1 *(Continued)*

SECTION	SUB-SECTION
Emergency	— Policies
	* OPP 1.34 Provision for essential services
	— Procedures
	* OPP 2.52 Evacuation of personnel
	* PO-015 Equipment contingency plan
	* OPP 1.38 Bomb threat
	* PO-015.1 Elevator evacuation
	— Telephone numbers

THE TECHNICAL LIBRARY

The diversified nature of a physical plant operation necessitates the establishment of a library containing appropriate code books and technical publications. The library should include:

- a set of National Fire Codes
- a set of National Building Codes
- a set of local codes governing building systems and construction
- a National Electrical Code handbook
- a Life Safety Code handbook
- regulatory body requirements for systems and equipment
- reference manuals for the design, operation and maintenance of buildings systems
- a guide for the administration of real property
- manufacturers equipment manuals
- the buildings specification manual
- a handbook of engineering fundamentals
- handbooks on refrigeration and air conditioning, boilers and pressure vessels, illumination, air handling systems and fan control, electric motor and pumps, carpentry, plumbing and pipefitting, masonry, pneumatics and hydraulics, welding, plant maintenance and other topics specific to your operation
- an automotive encyclopedia

- technical dictionaries
- a copy of this book

THE QUALITY ASSURANCE PROGRAM

Managing a physical plant is an awesome endeavor. No one person can keep on top of all the activities and concerns associated with its operation for long, without a good set of checks and balances. A properly implemented QA program can provide the monitoring you need to guarantee the efficient use of manpower, the proper care of equipment, compliance with regulations and cost effective operation in your plant.

Your quality assurance program should include a criteria-based, written plan which emphasizes the identification and correction of problems on a continuous basis and insures against their recurrence. Problems are occurrences varying from an established norm. They can be specific or general in nature. You may want to assure that the operating logs are completed daily or that certain components of the PM program are strictly adhered to. You might want to monitor budget line item expenditures on a weekly basis or determine the frequency of alternation of your boiler's feed water pumps. Whatever you intend to scrutinize, your plan should include:

- a list of the items to be monitored
- key factors for each item
- the method used for monitoring the item
- criteria for evaluating the key factors
- forms for listing, analyzing and planning the resolution of problems found

Items of concern can be added to or deleted from the QA program as needed but it is good policy to frequently review and evaluate the program to determine its effectiveness as your priorities change.

PERSONNEL FILES

The single, most indispensable and unimpeachable source of information on individual employees is a personnel jacket. You can learn much about a person by thoroughly reviewing their files, as long as you realize that the data they contain is the result of often indifferent processing and opinionated clinical appraisal.

A complete personnel folder will contain:

- results of a pre-employment physical
- the original application/resume
- evidence of orientation to the department and corporation
- business and personal references
- transcripts from school attendance
- results of employment tests
- copies of certificates, licenses, diplomas, citations and recommendations pertaining to his work
- annual performance appraisals for each of the years he has worked there
- employee station assignments
- job description
- a list of seminars and conferences attended
- a summary of promotions within the company
- a listing of in-house training programs attended
- employee change orders showing pay increase dates and amounts
- union affiliations
- attendance records
- dates of layoffs and returns
- a summary of disciplinary actions
- sign-off sheets for policies and procedures
- sign-off sheets for tools, keys, books and special clothing

CLERICAL ASSISTANCE

Whether you are blessed with a secretary, maintenance clerk, some combination of the two, or you use a supervisor to do your leg work, you must delegate the more mundane tasks associated with your position if you ever expect to accomplish anything.

Typical duties of a clerical assistant include:

- typing correspondence
- answering the telephone
- making appointments
- scheduling vacations
- passing on messages
- screening walk-ins
- processing work requisitions
- taking meeting minutes
- making travel and hotel reservations
- maintaining office files and records
- creating work schedules
- preparing reports
- collecting and collating information

- preparing requests for quotations
- establishing and updating price lists
- ordering materials
- creating forms
- searching for parts
- tabulating expenses
- making copies
- preparing operating instructions
- posting certificates
- preparing purchase orders
- monitoring inventories
- updating manuals
- running errands

VENDOR FILES

A complete list of all vendors doing or having done business with your organization should be readily available and contain at least the following:

- name and address
- existing contracts
- local, toll free and emergency telephone numbers
- contacts and titles
- hours and days of operation
- services available
- summary of product line
- discounting available

- normal lead time
- minimum order quantities
- service history
- notations of part problems

OPERATING LOGS

Figures 8-2 and 8-3 are typical of the forms used in power plants for recording equipment readings. When thoroughly and properly completed, they supply a wealth of information concerning your operation without your ever having to set foot in the machinery spaces. Copies of the forms you use should be filled in by each shift operator and sent to your office for review the following morning. By the time you finish your first cup of coffee, you'll already have an idea as to how things went the night before.

Along with the equipment forms, your operators and for that matter, your security personnel, should be required to chronologically narrate their activities in a permanently bound and sequentially numbered log book. During your daily tour of the facility, you should take time to read their entries. The information you derive from the log books will provide you with still further insight into what was occurring in your absence.

MANAGEMENT ACTION PLANS

As a loss prevention consultant for many years, I was constantly amazed at the number of physical plant directors who managed by crisis, often times putting out fires while I was sitting in their offices. No they weren't firefighters, they were just disorganized and because of a lack of planning, were overwhelmed by the day-to-day problems that surfaced in their operations. Those who realized the error of their ways and developed a planning strategy now run successful operations; those who didn't might very well be firemen today. I know they are no longer managers.

You should have both a long-range plan that integrates with the overall mission of the corporation of which your department is part and parcel and a short-range plan such as the one depicted in Ap-

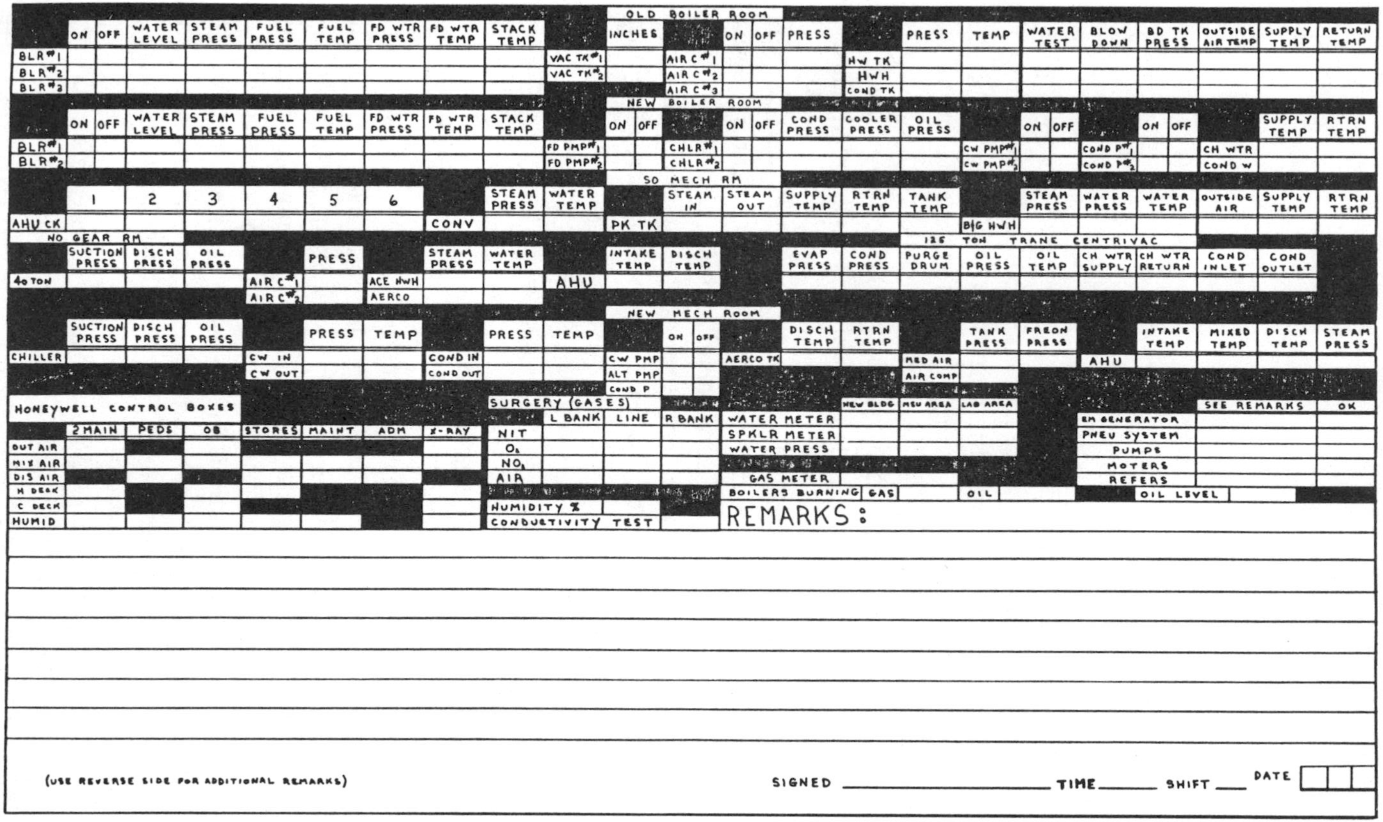

Figure 8-2. Equipment Operating Log.

PLANT OPERATIONS

10/84

EMERGENCY GENERATOR OPERATING LOG

Date	RUN TIME		TANK LEVEL		LOADING			TEST ABORT		REASON
	Start	End	Day	Fuel	Sim	Outage	Full	Yes	No	

PRE-START

OIL LEVEL		BATTERY		FUEL TANK	COOLANT LEVEL		FILTERS		OPERATION	
OK	?	SG.	Lev.	Gallons	OK	?	Air	Oil	Hours	Last Date

OPERATING

VOLTS	CYCLES	AMPERES			WATER	OIL	FUEL	INDICATORS			TIME LAG			
		Leg. 1	Leg 2	Leg 3	Temp	PSI	PSI	Oil	Air	TS-1	TS-2	TS-3	TS-4	

POST-TEST

OIL LEVEL		BATTERY		FUEL TANK	COOLANT LEVEL		FILTERS		OPERATION	
OK	?	SG.	Lev.	Gallons	OK	?	Air	Oil	Hours	Diff

REMARKS

_____

_____

OPERATOR SIGNATURE _____

Figure 8-3. Equipment Operating Log.

pendix B, the objectives of which being more department specific. The plan should be goal oriented, made flexible to allow for priority changes and constantly monitored and updated. A one-year window should be continuously maintained.

EQUIPMENT HISTORY FILES

Just as you maintain a personnel jacket on each of the people that works for you, a history file should be kept on every system and piece of equipment that works for you—your mechanical employees if you will.

The files should provide a complete history of their service, from installation through salvaging and include:

- the item name and house number
- serial and model numbers
- location and use
- system identification
- manufacturer
- warranty
- vendor name purchased from
- purchase price
- date and cost of installation
- date put into service
- lubrication and testing requirements
- service area
- reference to parts and repair manuals
- nameplate data
- equipment specifications
- state and municipal numbers
- reference to building plans and drawings
- chronological narrative of repairs
- chronological listing of parts replacement

- dates of inspections and findings
- reference to preventive maintenance performed
- labor and material expenditures
- insurance coverage
- parts stocked
- cost of removal

REDUCED-SCALE DRAWINGS

Several complete sets of reduced, scaled-as-built drawings should be available for conceptualizing renovations or modifications to building structures and systems, to communicate information about existing layouts to other departments and outside vendors, as an aid in orienting personnel to specific locations of equipment and system extensions and quick dimensioning of spaces and openings for engineering calculations.

COMPUTERIZATION

The paperwork generated within a physical plant can rival the bureaucracy of some small governments. Unless the manager controls the output, distribution and retention of printed materials within his organization, he will be consumed by it. The paper dinosaurs we have grown accustomed to are nearing extinction as we are required to provide larger volumes of more precise information to higher numbers of people, due to governmental regulation, economic operating constraints and our need to keep abreast of our own operations.

Although the use of computers in our field is only limited by our imaginations and the restraints of our budgets, we primarily rely on them for energy management, equipment control and generating reports. As a management aid, even a modest investment in a small personal computer and some select software will enable you to track, correlate and document a high volume of diversified information.

A PC should provide you with the capability to:

- track labor and material expenditures for maintenance cost charge backs to individual cost centers

- track repairs by trade to establish staffing needs and standard hours

- compile equipment histories for determining life expectancies and making repair/replacement decisions

- list deferred jobs and work backlogs for re-assignment

- list part numbers and costs of all frequently used, unstocked spares and their par levels

- list stocked material par levels, reorder points and costs

- schedule and record results of fire warning systems pull station/ heat detectors, fire pump and sprinkler flow tests

- schedule monthly fire extinguisher inspections and fire drills

- track electrical safety tests on new equipment and inspections on all electrical receptacles and distribution systems.

- monitor the daily analysis program for boiler and cooling tower waters and chemical usage

- track meter readings for comparison to billing for water, sewage, electric, natural gas and fuel oil consumption

- construct multiple letters of request for quotation and rejection for vendors

- construct and update policies and procedures

- type and update reports

- design forms used in the department

- track ordered parts and materials

- assign, track and document results of PM schedules for physical plant equipment

- monitor outside contracts

- establish valve and switch lists

- store and retrieve survey information when requested by outside agencies

- provide a cross reference of vendor contracts and manufacturers index file of parts and maintenance manuals

THE MANAGER'S DIARY

Plant directors are bombarded with questions and must make decisions from the time they set foot on the properties they manage. Unless you are blessed with total recall, you are bound to forget something that was brought to your attention during the course of a day. Some managers carry small paper pads with them, into which they make notes throughout the day. Most accumulate piles of notes on loose scratch paper in their pockets which, upon review at the end of the day, make no sense to them whatsoever. Others don't even go through the trouble of writing anything down at all.

You should purchase a bound, hardback annual calendar which has plenty of space in it for notation. It can be used to enter:

- meeting times and dates
- reminders of things to do
- vendor appointments
- notes on equipment problems
- questions requiring research
- dates for planned outages
- notes on inspector's findings
- completion dates of important projects
- summaries of each day's activities

The book can thus serve as a permanent record for constructing activity reports and reviewing the year's operation.

Chapter 9
DEPARTMENT OPERATIONS

Once established, the support items we just discussed will better enable you to address the operating considerations we are about to. If properly implemented and maintained these items can be added to your coterie of management aids.

BUDGETS

The wheels of industry don't turn because we lubricate them; they move as the result of heavy applications of money. Like oil, money is a finite resource which must be conserved and used wisely. The budgeting process is our means to that end. For our purposes, we must prepare three separate and distinct budgets to cover the department's man-hours, department operating expenses and capital equipment and projects expenditures.

The Table of Contents displayed in Figure 9-1 lists the worksheets, notes and reports typically used in projecting and justifying a departmental budget.

The LABOR HOURS section is used for establishing department manpower needs for the coming year. The workload volume forecast lists the total productive man-hours required, plans for non-productive hours such as vacations and holidays, anticipates non-productive hours such as sick time, lists current staffing as full-time equivalents (FTE) and forecasts total paid hours for the coming year in monthly increments. The staffing profile acts as a worksheet for estimating required manhours by function within each position and forms the basis for comparison of projected to existing manpower needs.

The section entitled OPERATING BUDGET accounts for all departmental expenditures other than those that are capitalized. The line item totals describes the line items, lists their cost center numbers and system input codes and provides a total budgeted dollar

Figure 9-1. Table of Contents; Budget Workbook

SECTION	PAGE
Labor hours	
* Workload volume forecast	1
* Staffing profile	2-8
Operating Budget	
* Line item totals	9-15
* Worksheets	
– budget comparisons	16, 17
– salaries and wages	18
– purchased services	19
– department supplies	20
– utilities expense	21, 22
– repairs and maintenance	23-25
– pm contracts	26
– inspection/licenses	27
– travel & entertainment/professional development	28
Capital Budget	
* Equipment acquisitions	29-36
* Projects	37-51
Budget Notes	
* Problems and comments	52-56

figure for each item broken down into amounts reflective of those anticipated for the months in which the figures are allocated. The worksheets substantiate the total dollar figures for each line item. See Appendix C for an example of an operating budget for a small physical plant.

The CAPITAL BUDGET section of the workbook includes justification for purchases of new equipment and high expense projects which qualify by corporate definition as capital expenditures.

Problems and comments concerning your budget can be listed in the BUDGET NOTES section for reference by and discussion with your controller or CEO.

REQUESTS FOR QUOTATIONS

Congratulations! Your budgets have been approved. Let's spend some of the money you've worked so diligently to acquire. Unfortunately the budget committee has hacked away at your proposals until they no longer resemble your original submission. You will have to rethink your ideas on how to accomplish the things you had planned to do. It's eerie how much this sounds like a letter of rejection but don't despair; we can work it out.

You have been put into a position that requires you to get the best value for the dollars you spend. Whether you are buying supplies or contracting for service, comparative shopping and competitive bids will help to keep your budget variances in line.

Never make a significant purchase or enter into a contractural agreement before first requesting quotations from at least three different vendors. Formalizing your request and requiring a minimum of three submissions:

- forces you to set down your ideas in writing
- allows you time to think through your plans and alter them if necessary
- provides you with competitive pricing
- enables your input into the wording of subsequent agreements
- allows you to control the situation

The request for quotation in Appendix D was written with these thoughts in mind.

The project called for the demolition and removal of several old building structures. Quotes were received from seven contractors, with a range of $195,000.00 between the highest and lowest bids. Each contractor was bidding from the same RFQ, agreeing to all of its conditions and stipulations. Since the contractor chosen was not involved in specifying the work, control of the project reverted to the owner. The contract was awarded to the lowest bidder, not slanted in any way on the contractor's behalf and was written almost verbatim from the RFQ.

WORK ORDER SYSTEMS

The need for having work accomplished can be communicated in many ways depending on the scope of the work and who is requesting it. Preventive maintenance is performed to a scheduled frequency.

The need for corrective maintenance can be conveyed via the telephone, a list prepared by a roundsman during his tour of the building or work requisition chits that form part of a work order system. Special project work such as equipment installations and building renovations call for their own set of documents to initiate and record job completion.

However the request is transmitted, it is imperative that you always control the accomplishment of the task from its inception through its completion and maintain your right to defer or disapprove the work during the requisitioning process. A work order system such as the one outlined in Appendix E should be established which will enable you to organize, prioritize, assign and document work done by your department personnel. If properly implemented, a system such as that will keep your telephone from ringing off the wall, appease the persons for whom the work is being performed and provide you feedback for determining staffing levels and material inventory levels.

CONTRACTS

Whole volumes have been written on the subject of contractual agreement to the extent that a separate field of law has been established to address it. The intent here is not to educate you in the paralegal aspects of contract law but rather to alert you to the pitfalls which could entrap you in contracting for services in support of your operation.

Generally speaking, a contract is a promise made by one party whch is supported by consideration from a second party. For instance; the elevator company promises to provide certain PM and repair services in return for an agreed upon dollar amount. The contract sets the terms and conditions that must be adhered to by both parties, the extent of the services to be provided and a schedule of payment. In this case, the contract was probably written by the elevator company and agreed to by the physical plant manager.

Unfortunately, unless you have the luxury of first passing contracts through your corporate legal beagles, you will find that most agreements you enter into will be written by and on behalf of the company with which you are negotiating. But that need not be. The magic word here is negotiate. You hold the purse strings which, for our purposes, is what consideration is all about. They know that they are not the only company making promises. This equation puts you in a superior position and gives you the power to make demands on them.

Granted, in the beginning you may be a bit timid in asserting yourself but you don't have to accomodate the whims of the vendors. Written contracts are not set in concrete. They can be amended or completely rewritten. Labor plus material contracts can be changed to fixed cost contracts or capped by a not-to-exceed figure. Payment schedules can be revised to eliminate up-front money and require specific levels of performance before payment or even partial payment is made. Cost increases caused by change orders can be avoided. You can call the shots. Just as you are bound by the verbage in the contract, so are they. Remember, you are out to get the best bang for your buck and you don't have to be a lawyer to do it. Negotiate.

REPORTS

Who needs to know what? Reporting on your operations is a time consuming activity. It is imperative that you supply sufficient information for the record but for purposes of confidentiality and constructive use of your time, it is also important that you provide only the needed data to the appropriate people within and outside of your organization.

So, what information should you convey? That depends on the type, size and scope of your department and organization, regulatory requirements and municipal ordinances under whose auspices you fall, corporate policy on data distribution and your individual need for retention of information within your department. Generic to all physical plants is the need to tabulate man-hour and dollar expenditures to monitor and explain variances in the department's budget. Although this mechanism provides a wealth of information on its own, it by no means tells the whole story of your operation. Reports should be generated on an established frequency which will:

- describe recent activities within your department
- explain the current status of projects
- refer to important correspondence
- state training received by personnel

- analyze department productivity
- break down material and labor cost for work performed
- monitor the PM work system
- summarize inspection findings
- track utility usage
- ascertain conformance with regulatory body requirements
- re-establish departmental priorities
- address past problems
- project future needs

EQUIPMENT ACQUISITION

From time to time you will purchase equipment for the plant. Other departments will also do some purchasing; some with your knowledge and some not.

The peculiar thing about installing it is that the new equipment doesn't always fit where the old units were, sometimes requiring extreme modification to existing systems and structures. Often times, during construction of a building, larger devices such as boilers and generators are set in place and the walls built up around them; kind of like building an airplane in your basement. Imagine the problems entailed in replacing them in your building.

Generally, little thought is ever given to installation and repair during the purchasing process. All the user knows is that he wants a particular unit, orders it and cries the blues when it can't be used immediately after it arrives. It then becomes our responsibility to make it work.

To save them from embarrassment and you from adding to your ulcer bank, a set of corporate guidelines for new equipment purchases should be established and strictly enforced. Prior to placement of an order for new equipment, the Plant Operations department should be consulted if one or more of the following conditions is involved.

- connection into any existing system
- the necessity for establishing a new system
- construction of new structures

- destruction or modification of the building proper
- the need for preventive maintenance on or testing of the devices

Prior to issuing an approved purchase order, the purchasing department should be required to submit manufacturer's test data and specifications to your department for review as well as plans for the disposition of the units being replaced. Once received, the equipment should be inspected and tested if necessary before being sent to the user department and determination of the need for a service contract or inclusion into the preventive maintenance program should be finalized prior to installation.

As a condition of purchase, the manufacturer should be required to supply you with:

- two operating manuals
- two performance specifications
- a full set of schematics
- one parts list
- one service manual
- warranty information
- recommended service schedules
- references to known hazards
- a certificate of liability insurance covering leased equipment

One copy of the operating manual should be sent to the user department, the insurance certificate sent to the corporate risk manager and the remainder of the information maintained in the Plant Operations department files. All purchase orders should contain a notation to notify the Plant Operations department upon receipt of all equipment and an electrical safety check should be performed on all electrically energized equipment before being released to the user department.

Chapter 10
PERSONNEL CONSIDERATIONS

Many of us hate to admit it but we are only as good as our people are. A scroll of our credentials could be as long as a child's Christmas wish list but our qualifications are assessed through the work performed by our employees. If we surround ourselves with competent personnel who always get the job done, properly and on time, we will be perceived as competent ourselves. If our personnel lack proper skills or initiative, we will be considered poor leaders and incapable of managing. None of us is fully blessed with the best or cursed with the worst. We are in a position, however, to mold our people to fit into either group. How successful we are in educating and motivating them is the true test of our management ability. Ninety-nine percent of how well we fare in our dealings with employees on the job, has to do with the communications skills we possess and our willingness to consistently apply them. How well we manage what follows comprises the remainder.

THE SCREENING PROCESS

Most companies subscribe to preordained hiring practices by policy. Their standard employment applications are not department or job specific since they are used throughout the company and pre-employment testing of applicants by the personnel department doesn't always work. How do you find the right people to fill all the different positions in your department?

If you're an expert in every trade, that won't be a problem for you but you're not. None of us is. I know it's hard to admit but come down from your ivory tower; none of us is expected to be. Yes, I know you worked in construction while you were in college and you operated refrigeration equipment in a cold storage plant and . . . you're missing the point. Would you feel comfortable interviewing journeymen mechanics and tradesmen to fill all of your department's positions? If you can honestly answer yes to that question you don't need my help or anyone else's for that matter. In you're like me, you can use all the help you can get. So how do we go about it?

Personnel departments do have some redeeming qualities. Their employment applications provide enough information to eliminate applicants who obviously do not qualify for the positions you are trying to fill. After explaining the minimum requirements you'll accept, your personnel department can save you a lot of time and grief by thoroughly screening applicants for you. They can research their work backgrounds, check personal and business references, determine academic achievement and summarize any special skills they may possess. As the result of screening, you might then be confronted with ten candidates instead of four hundred applicants. The requirement levels you set determine how many candidates you will see. Establish realistic parameters based on available manpower from the community from which you expect to draw the candidates. If you set a goal too high to attain, you may only be talking to yourself. Remember, you can train them after they're hired.

So you have four candidates for the Stationary Engineer's position, three for the Carpenter Foreman position and three for the Head Electrician's position. Are you going to interview them? Ultimately you will interview every person who eventually becomes a part of your organization, but should you be the one to determine their qualifications? Do we have to review your work background again? Wasn't your maintenance supervisor a Stationary Engineer? Didn't George build houses for a living before becoming a maintenance foreman in your department? Okay, you get the picture. Let those men further screen the candidates for you. If your people think they are qualified, then they probably are. Your job will be to determine how well the candidates will fit in with the rest of your group. Don't feel put down, personnel is sending over a candidate for the refrigeration mechanic's position next week and he's all yours.

It is unlawful to ask a potential employee certain questions regarding race, color, religion, sex, national origin, age, handicaps . . . and the list goes on and on. Before taking on the chore of interviewing candidates for a position, make certain you understand the significance of that statement and get some tutoring on the subject. What seems like an innocent question to you might be grounds for litigation to a court judge.

Be careful but don't be afraid. For every question you can't ask, there are a thousand that you can. A good rule of thumb is to ask only questions relevant to the position you are filling. Much can be gained by asking no questions at all. If you can get the person started on a subject, sit back and let him do the talking. Before beginning, arrange to have your messages intercepted and take your telephone off of the hook. Concentrate one hundred percent on the interview.

During the interview, pay special attention to any written materials the candidate has provided you. Was there much thought put into its construction? Is it neat? Does it appear accurate and logical? Give the candidate a visual going over. Is he dressed appropriately for the interview? Does he display good grooming? Weigh other factors, as well. Does he seem intelligent? Does he have a good attitude?

Share a job description with him and discuss each duty listed. Have him discuss similar duties he has performed for other employers. Does he appear knowledgeable on each subject? Pose a hypothetical problem and ask him how he would resolve it. Was his response logical and authoritative?

The atmosphere you provide has a great bearing on how successful the interview will be. Try to keep the proceedings on an informal basis and don't resort to trick questions. Be honest and don't try to psychoanalyze every answer you get. Keep it simple and to the point. It hasn't been so long since you were in the hot seat on the other side of the desk. Remember how you felt and give the guy a break.

After the interview the screening process continues. You may want to discuss the candidate's qualifications with your supervisors or even call them back for additional interviews. Your company may require pre-employment physicals. After hiring them, the probationary period serves as a screening tool in determining if they will remain on as employees. Even if they make it through their probationary periods, they must pass the scrutiny of their supervisors daily and do well on their annual performance appraisals. A person may be hired as a full-time employee but there is no such thing as a permanent position.

EMPLOYEE ORIENTATION

Many managers make the mistake of hiring a person and putting them immediately to work. Assuming that we've gone to great lengths in checking these people out and we expect them to be with us for awhile, doesn't it make sense to make them part of the team? If you stick him down in the boiler room, you will isolate him from the rest of the operation and although he may become your best operator, he will quickly fall into a routine of putting in his eight hours and punching out on time. If you take some time with him up front to orient him to the total operation, he will better understand what is expected of him and feel more like a member of the group. People tend to contribute more when interest is shown in them and contribution equals productivity.

Okay, I sold you on the concept. So how do you go about orienting this guy? Depending on how much information you wish to convey to the person, a block of time should be set aside which is consistently the same for all new hires. A schedule should be made indicating the times allocated for him to absorb the various topics that will be presented or discussed. You, yourself, should be available to answer questions that may arise during the course of his orientation. Minimally the orientation should include the following:

- a brief tour of the entire facility
- historical background on the company
- an in-depth tour of the area where he will perform his work
- a review of the company's policies
- introduction to key people in the organization
- your expectations of his performance
- a personnel handbook covering benefits, grievance procedures and disciplinary action
- an outline of his job responsibilities and duties
- an explanation of the performance evaluation process

STANDARDS OF PERFORMANCE

People in subordinate positions tend to emulate their superiors. Just as the manager is no better than his people are, his people will prove no better than he. Your example sets the standards of performance in your operation. If you are lax in enforcing discipline, your supervisors will overlook employee indiscretions. If you spend a lot of time around the water cooler, your men will take extended coffee breaks. Say, while we're at it, why don't we have a cup? We've been discussing the operation to death and we both need a break.

Thanks, There is a plus side to the performance issue. If you are professional in all of your dealings, your people will act professionally. If they know you aren't asking them to do something you wouldn't do yourself, they'll respect you for it. If you show good judgment in your decisions, it will rub off on them. Look at the operation through their eyes and you'll soon see what I'm saying.

PERFORMANCE EVALUATIONS

Unfortunately, the performance evaluation is a greatly misunderstood and underutilized tool of management. In large operations it is relegated to annual use by managers in determining pay increases or as a disciplining vehicle for troublesome employees. Except for a brief exchange of pleasantries as they pass in the corridor, an employee's performance evaluation may be his only forum for conversing with the director of his department. What good are they?

A tool is only as effective as the person using it. On its own and of itself it performs no work. It only supplies the potential for constructive use. In the right hands a hammer can be used to build a shelter. Improperly used it can tear down the sturdiest of structures. Like a hammer, a performance appraisal can be used constructively or maliciously. The evaluation process entails more than an appraisal of an employee's performance. It is also an opportunity for management to spend quality time with him to discuss concerns and expectations you both may have, clarify your position on dealings with him and plan for his development over the long haul. You can use the time to build his confidence and fortify his committment or to tear away at his character. It's your hammer.

Corporate policy may require you to annually evaluate each employee in your department but probably will not limit you to that frequency. Nowhere will it state that you can't speak with them more often. Granted, you don't need to use a written form each time you converse with them and at times it may be preferable to use none at all, but when you do, it should be more than just a checklist. The queries contained on the form should provoke discussion of the issues being addressed. What do you feel is your role in the department? Where would you like to be five years from now? How can the operation be improved upon? What are your greatest concerns? Open communications with your employees promotes understanding and comradery in the physical plant. If your people aren't talking with you, they are talking about you. How and if you choose to communicate determines what is being said. The evaluation process is one of several options open to you for communicating with your personnel.

JOB DESCRIPTIONS

Who's responsible for doing what? You are responsible for making certain every task in the plant is accomplished, properly and in a timely fashion. You determine what, when, how, where and by whom work is done. It stands to reason that you won't personally assign each individual task to be performed; after all that's the supervisor's responsibility, is it not? No, it is not. The supervisor assigns jobs, not tasks. Sure, there will be times when both you or he will assign particular tasks as the need arises but that will be the exception, not the rule. For the most part, work in the physical plant is accomplished by the workforce to sets of guidelines called job descriptions.

Job descriptions can be simple lists of duties to be performed by individuals in the course of their work, ornate sets of instructions detailing the minutest aspects of a position or anything in between. Their purpose should be to provide a base of understanding for the worker as regards his position and responsibilities within the organization. Job descriptions are actually position descriptions. They are statements of the duty requirements of titled positions; not work assignments for the persons filling them. As such, they cannot vary from person to person within a given classification and consistency in their application is assured.

Every position and level within a position warrants that a separate description be written for each. All job descriptions should contain at least the following information about the positions they describe:

- the position title and level
- the scope of the position
- to whom the position reports
- the holder's authority
- required qualifications
- a detailed list of duties
- the author's name and title
- appropriate approval signatures
- the effective date
- employee recognition signature

As no job description, however comprehensive, can anticipate every conceivable future circumstance, it is wise to include a statement in its construction indicating that the duties in its text are a summarization of the responsibilities associated with the position and are not intended to address every task the holder may be called upon to complete. A notation such as this can belay many arguments you may otherwise encounter should your employee try to use his job description as a defense against inferior performance.

Chapter 11
PROJECT WORK

Work, work, work. Not only do we have a lot of it but there are so many different kinds of it. Sometimes it seems we have more jobs than we have people to handle them. Our mechanics take care of the preventive maintenance, operation and troubleshooting of our equipment. Our maintenance people facilitate building repairs. Our secretaries take care of the paper work. Who do we have left to do the renovations? To hell with the coffee, let's go out and discuss this matter over a cold beer. There are few perquisites associated with our position, but taking advantage of the chance to get away once in a while to clear your mind is one I highly recommend.

ASSEMBLING THE TROOPS

How do you like the place? Sure, I eat here often. It belongs to a former building manager who developed ulcers from working sixteen-hour days. Did you bring your notebook? Good, let's get started.

The trouble with project work is that no two jobs are ever alike. Like ulcers, they come in all shapes and sizes; some you must give serious consideration to while others are easily remedied. By its nature, project work is a one-shot deal that requires staffing only until the work has been completed. There are times when you'll have projects scheduled back-to-back for months on end then have slack periods upwards of a year where no major work needs to be performed. How should you staff your department to accomodate these inconsistencies? Do you hire on full-time personnel in anticipation of the work? What happens when the project is cancelled out? Do you hire a full-time crew on a temporary basis? Good people are hard to come by unless you offer them more secure employment. Do you use contractors? Depending on the scope of the project this may become necessary but bear in mind you'll pay a premium for the luxury of hiring outside help. Can you use existing staff personnel? The truth is, your staff should be capable of handling all but the most involved projects confronting your department.

To a lesser degree, the knowledge needed for maintaining your building and systems is essentially the same as the knowledge required to construct and install them. Constructing a building may entail the need for employing a contractor but renovations and small additions can be tackled in-house. The installation of a complex system may warrant the hiring of outside help but the modification of a system may be accomplishable by your personnel. You can assemble a team from your ranks to complete a given project just as you would a baseball team to compete against a given opponent. Your team members remain the same but the line-up will change to accommodate the project.

When department personnel double as construction crews you save on the cost of premium wages to outside vendors, you avoid the hiring and lay-off process and your people take pride in accomplishing the work themselves. The choice to use them in this way is yours, barring any restrictions that may be imposed upon you by a bargaining agreement. Just remember to change their job descriptions before attempting to change their jobs.

ORGANIZING THE FILES

How to document your projects is a singular decision. If you haven't got an inkling as to where to begin, here are a few ideas.

Projects can generate an inordinate amount of paperwork. Before beginning any project, make certain you have sufficient file space to control it. The number and scope of the projects you take on will dictate what space is needed. It is advisable to devote at least an entire file cabinet to project documents and its drawers should separate projects by status as pending, in progress or completed. Much of the supporting documentation associated with project work, such as purchase orders and invoices, is redundant to your normal operation and as such should remain there but copied to the project folder for purposes of reference. Other information normally found in a project file includes:

- planning scenarios and photographs
- vendor contracts, bonds and insurance certificates
- building permits
- correspondence
- minutes from project meetings
- architectural and engineering renderings
- work schedules
- progress reports
- guarantees and warranties
- change orders and punch lists
- equipment manuals
- material specifications
- approvals

VISUALIZING THE JOB

So you have plenty of empty file cabinets, your men are anxious to take on a project and your secretary is standing by for instructions. Good. Call your secretary and tell her to have the men move the cabinets to your office then return to their normal routines. You have a lot to consider before involving them. Who needs what done? What do they have in mind? Whose budget will the project be charged against? Are there alternatives to the proposed work? How will it affect the overall operation? How big is the job?

After these and a thousand other questions have been asked in establishing a need, you must then investigate the feasability of filling the need before gaining tentative approval to proceed.

With a clear understanding of the end result in mind, you should visit the site of the intended work and learn as much about its physical characteristics as possible in order to determine its potential. When you arrive you should have in your possession all of the tools you will need to make an accurate assessment of what is there. Your kit may include:

- a camera loaded with self-developing film
- maps and drawings of the area
- binoculars for studying details of high or distant structures
- a pen and clipboard for making sketches
- a tape recorder for making notes
- a 100-foot tape for taking measurements
- a stepladder for access into ceilings
- a flashlight for obvious reasons

Everyone has their own ideas on what to take to the job site with them. Some use heat guns, stethoscopes and infrared cameras. Some take along volt-ohm meters and wooden stakes. Whatever you choose as appropriate for surveying the site is fine but you'll find that the most effective tool in this situation will be a good set of ears connected to an open mind. Take along a person or group of people who have knowledge and experience in what you're trying to accomplish. They can provide you with valuable input which can save you from making unnecessary expenditures, wasting time and duplicating your efforts. Besides, you weren't planning to carry all that stuff yourself, were you?

THE PLANNING PROCESS

Projects can be likened to football games in that they both require game plans to insure their success. In the project game, you are the general manager, your supervisors are the coaches and your personnel are the players. As usual, the owner is relegated to picking up the tab. If a project can be equated to a game, then all the projects completed in a year constitute a season. How well you conceive and implement your individual game plans determines whether you end each season as a contender or as an also ran. Just as each opposing team poses a different challenge causing you to alter your game plan, each project presents special problems which cause you to modify your work plan for completing it. Whereas all teams have basic plans, only those whose plans are flexible enough to meet those challenges will wax victorious.

As I've just intimated, the diversity of project work precludes the consistent use of exacting plans. Whereas all project plans incorporate the same basic elements in their development, individual projects dictate the order and intensity of their application. Here is a checklist of some elements to consider before the coin toss:

- feasibility studies
- pre-plan discussions with affected departments
- selection of project team members
- hiring of sub-contractors
- negotiation of contracts
- narration of bid requests
- specification of materials, tools and techniques
- acquisition of required permits
- site preparation
- instruction and scheduling of personnel
- acceptability of change orders
- compliance with regulatory body requirements
- interruptions to operations
- completion dates and deadlines
- ordering of materials
- required approvals
- scheduling of progress meetings
- labor and material expenditures
- reuse of existing materials and structures
- inspections and tests
- maintenance of forms and records
- distribution of drawings
- insurance and bonding requirements
- demolition of existing structures
- job safety
- researching of building costs

- completion of punch lists
- phasing of project levels
- receiving and storing materials
- contingency planning
- using consultants
- securing the work site
- job clean-up
- temporary washroom facilities for the work crews
- coordination of utility hook-ups
- temporary structures for protection from the weather
- isolating the job site from the public
- designation of lead people
- consideration of design constraints
- mapping out of the mechanicals
- recourse for bad workmanship
- tolerability of substitutions

SALVAGE OPERATIONS

Most project work performed by your department will entail the modification of existing structures. New is nice, but it's not always the answer. There is intrinsic value in reworking portions of an old structure resulting in lower manpower requirements, less use of materials and enhancement of the structure's original character. Thought should be given to repairing and/or reusing:

- lock and passage sets
- door butts, panic hardware and closers
- exterior windows
- suspended ceiling grids
- plumbing fixtures
- built-in cabinetry
- railings and bannisters

- decorative stone
- metal ducting and plenums
- decorative moulding
- air registers and diffusers
- fluorescent light fixtures

This technique must be administered selectively, for as much as you can gain from reusing some items, you can lose on others. Never reuse old electrical wiring and devices. The ashes that fall on the floor may be you. Never reuse old wooden supports. If you want to get to the basement quickly, use the elevator. Never reuse old sewage piping. The idea stinks; if you catch my drift. A good rule of thumb is to reuse only those things you will see when the job is finished. Let common sense be your guide.

Chapter 12
ASSESSMENT CRITERIA

After six months or so on the job, it's a good idea to step back and take a hard look at your operation to determine how it has progressed over that span of time; then semi-annually or annually thereafter. Upon reflection, take pride in and credit for things done well, keeping in mind those that were not. Performing an objective self-assessment from time to time enables a department to recognize areas needing improvement and provides a vehicle for adjusting its priorities to meet those needs. The department operation and your reputation are inextricably linked. How you choose to act on the facts you uncover has a direct bearing on the prestige you will enjoy as a manager.

When you evaluate your own performance you don't have to be religious to do your soul searching but what you find will sometimes put the fear of God in you. Wrapped up in the day-to-day operation, it's easy to lose sight of your original objectives. Even the best in-tentioned of us deviate from the plan to some extent. When you look into the mirror, be honest and prepare yourself for some shocking revelations. At best, it is difficult to accept criticism from others, but self-realization can be devastating. The character of your operation is an extension of your own. If you fare well, so will the operation. If you don't, farewell may be the next word you hear.

Appendix F is an example of a departmental self-assessment performed by a manager of a small physical plant after his first six months on the job. The criteria he used in its completion follow here.

THE ORGANIZATION

- The corporate and department organizational charts are current
- The Standard Operating Procedures is kept up to date

- Policies and/or procedures have been written to address all department concerns and are reviewed annually

THE MANAGER

- Frequent inspection tours of the building are made
- Other departments are kept informed of work progress
- All scheduled meetings are attended
- Long- and short-range plans are prepared and updated
- Inquiries are responded to personally and in a timely manner
- Quality time is spent with key people in the organization
- Loyal concern for the corporation is always demonstrated
- A monthly department activities report is completed
- Frequent visits with second- and third-shift personnel are made
- All department forms are properly filled out and maintained
- The operations of the other departments in the corporation are learned
- Keeps abreast of changes in his field
- Keeps on top of issues confronting the corporation
- The department's standards of performance are revised as needed
- Desks and files are kept neat and orderly
- Strict employee confidence is always maintained
- Daily planning meetings are held with supervisory personnel
- Projects are completed in a timely and cost effective manner
- A system exists for prioritizing all work requests

PERSONNEL

- All new personnel are orientated to corporate and department policy
- Each employee has read and signed a current job description
- A full staff of qualified people is maintained in the department

- Each employee receives an annual written performance evaluation
- Training sessions are provided to upgrade employee skills
- Records are maintained on employee non-productive time
- Monthly work schedules are posted in the department
- A complete personnel file is maintained on each employee
- Department meetings are held regularly and minutes kept
- Copies of all professional licenses are kept on file
- Work is always matched to the person assigned to complete it
- The dress code is strictly adhered to

DOCUMENTATION

- All logs and service records are completed on time
- All blueprints are current and each set is complete
- Forms used in the department are current
- An inventory is performed annually on all parts, materials and tools stocked by the department
- All work orders are scrutinized through completion
- Records are kept on all preventive maintenance work performed and equipment history cards are constantly updated
- A personnel jacket is maintained on all employees
- Time cards and wage rates are monitored

FINANCES

- Labor and material costs for all work performed are tabulated, recorded and compared with initial estimates
- All requests for salary increases are reviewed by the manager
- Budget variances are always justified and department expenditures are approved by the manager
- Invoices are always reviewed and paid on time

- An energy conservation program exists and is enforced
- The status of all purchase orders is constantly monitored
- Utility expenditures are tracked monthly

BUILDINGS AND GROUNDS

- All areas of the building are kept well lit
- Emergency lighting is maintained throughout the building
- Rounds routines are current and monitored
- Machinery spaces are kept clean and uncluttered
- Evacuation drills are performed according to corporate policy
- Records are kept on the fire rating of all materials used
- The premises are always kept clear of trash and debris
- The ways of travel are kept in good repair
- All exits are kept clear of snow and ice
- All walls, floors and ceilings are well maintained
- All lights are in working order
- All doors function properly
- All blinds and windows are maintained in good repair
- All electrical receptacles and switches are maintained
- All plumbing fixtures work properly
- All building and system leaks are immediately corrected
- Parking lots and drives are kept in good repair
- No broken glass is found anywhere in the building

EQUIPMENT AND SYSTEMS

- All equipment is covered by the preventive maintenance program
- Operating certificates are prominently posted in the machinery space where the equipment is located
- The valve and switch lists are updated annually

- All panels, valves and switches are labeled for the areas they serve
- All required inspections and tests are performed and recommendations are complied with
- An inventory of consumable PM items is maintained
- A color code has been implemented for all systems
- All main shut-off valves and switches are labeled for quick identification during emergencies
- The fire warning system is tested frequently
- Written operating procedures are posted by all mechanical devices
- The emergency generator is frequently tested under load
- Proper tools are provided and maintained for all work performed
- Adequate spare parts are stocked to ensure uninterrupted operation of all equipment and systems
- All water contents are kept within prescribed parameters
- A schedule of steam trap repair is maintained
- Emmissions from equipment are monitored

SAFETY

- All fire extinguishers have tags that are signed when inspected
- All safety rules are posted prominently within the department
- Emergency telephone call lists are kept updated
- There is a current disaster procedures manual
- The electrical safety program is reviewed annually
- All personnel are familiar with fire procedures
- Flammable materials are always stored in approved fire cabinets or rooms constructed to house such materials
- Safety gear is provided for use in all hazardous areas
- All employees are familiar with back-up procedures when major systems are lost or disrupted
- All equipment is kept properly shielded

- Equipment undergoing repairs is prominently tagged out of service

You can use these criteria as a base for establishing your own parameters for self assessment. As time passes and your priorities change, you can add to or delete from the list. Once your list is complete, how you go about applying them is entirely up to you.

In the example assessment, each criterion was referenced and general observations were noted when problems became evident. Specific details regarding the observations were then started and conclusions were derived concerning the problems found. Recommendations were made and a time frame for their completion was established. The system you use to evaluate your operation is not the issue here. The proper operation of your system is.

I hope my input has been of some help to you. Good luck with your first appraisal. Let's have the girls get together and we'll have dinner. I'm out of here.

Appendix A

STATE OF OHIO
STATIONARY STEAM ENGINEERS
AND BOILER OPERATORS
LICENSE LAWS

INDEX

STEAM ENGINE   An engine in which the mechanical force arising from the elasticity and expansive action of steam, or from its property of rapid condensation, or from a combination of the two, is made available as a motive power. Century Dictionary

SECTION 4739.01 (1040). ADMINISTRATION

Sections 4739.01 to 4739.15, inclusive, of the Revised Code, relating to the chief examiner of steam engineers, shall be administered by the chief of division of examiners of steam engineers as created under section 121.04 of the Revised Code.

As used in sections 4739.01 to 4739.15, inclusive, of the Revised Code, "Chief examiner of steam engineers" means the chief of the division of examiners of steam engineers. The chief examiner of steam engineers shall divide the state into ten districts. With the approval of the governor he shall appoint an assistant chief examiner and ten district examiners of steam engineers, each of whom shall be a competent and practical steam engineer, from a list of applicants who have successfully passed an appropriate civil service examination. Upon the resignation, removal, or death of the chief examiner, assistant chief examiner, or a district examiner, the vacancy shall be filled in the manner provided for the original appointment. (Effective September 23, 1969)

SECTION 4739.02 (1041). QUALIFICATIONS

The chief examiner of steam engineers shall be a practical steam engineer of not less than ten years' experience. The assistant chief examiner and each district examiner of steam engineers shall be a practical steam engineer of not less than seven years' experience.

SECTION 4739.03 (1045). ACCESS TO BUILDINGS

To make an examination or inspection authorized by law, the chief examiner of steam engineers and each district examiner may enter upon any premises and into any building or room thereof at all reasonable hours.

SECTION 4739.04 (1047). HORSEPOWER DEFINED

No person shall operate a stationary steam boiler or engine of more than thirty horsepower without obtaining a license. A horsepower means twelve square feet of boiler heating surface. No owner or user or agent of an owner or user of any such steam boiler or engine shall permit it to be operated unless it is directly in the charge of a licensed engineer.

SECTION 4739.05 (1048). LICENSE APPLICATION; RULES

Each person who desires to act as a steam engineer shall make application to the district examiner of steam engineers for a license, upon a blank furnished him, and shall pass an examination in the construction and operation of steam boilers, steam engines, and steam pumps, and in the subject of hydraulics. Examination questions shall pertain only to the practical operation of stationary steam engines, stationary steam boilers, and steam pumps. The examination shall be conducted under the rules and regulations adopted by the chief examiner which shall be uniform throughout the state. The district examiners, assistant chief examiner, and chief examiner may administer all oaths or affirmations to any applicant whenever the same is made necessary by the rules and regulations adopted by the chief examiner.

SECTION 4739.06 (1049). LICENSE AND REVOCATION

If, upon examination, the applicant is found proficient in the subject mentioned in section 4739.05 of the Revised Code a license shall be granted him to have charge of and operate station steam boilers and engines of the horsepower required by section 4739.04 of the Revised Code, for one year from the date on which it is issued. Upon written charges, after notice and hearing, the district examiner may revoke the license of a person guilty of fraud in obtaining such license, or who becomes insane, or is addicted to the liquor or drug habits to such a degree as to render him unfit to discharge the duties of a steam engineer.

Common pleas jurisdiction, 2305.01.

SECTION 4739.07 (1050). RENEWALS

Upon application, the person to whom a license is issued under section 4739.01 to 4739.10, inclusive, of the Revised Code, shall be entitled to a renewal thereof annually, unless the district examiner for a cause named in section 4739.06 of the Revised Code and upon notice and hearing shall refuse such renewal.

SECTION 4739.08 (1053). MUST EXHIBIT LICENSE

No steam engineer shall neglect or refuse to exhibit his license under glass in a conspicuous place in his engine room.

Penalty, 4739.99 (A)

SECTION 4739.09 (1056). PROHIBITION

No engineer, or owner, or user, or agent of an owner or user of a steam boiler or engine shall violate sections 4739.01 to 4739.10, inclusive, of the Revised Code.

Penalty, 4739.99 (B).

(Amended June 14, 1957).

SECTION 4739.10 (1057). EXCEPTIONS

Sections 4739.01 to 4739.10 inclusive, of the Revised Code do not apply to boilers and engines under the jurisdiction of the United States, or to locomotive boilers and engines nor to the owners or users thereof.

SECTION 4739.11 (1058-5). EXEMPTIONS

Sections 4739.04 of the Revised Code, insofar as it has relation to the operation and having charge of stationary steam boilers, shall not apply to persons holding license issued under sections 4739.11 to 4739.15, inclusive, of the Revised Code.

SECTION 4739.12 (1058-1). LICENSES

Any person who desires to operate or have charge of a stationary steam boiler of more than thirty horsepower, except boilers which are in charge of a licensed engineer, shall make application to the district examiner of steam engineers for a license upon a blank furnished by the examiner, and shall pass an examination on the construction and operation of steam boilers, steam pumps, and hydraulics, under such rules and regulations as may be adopted by the chief examiner of steam engineers, which rules and regulations and standard of examination shall be uniform throughout the state. Examination questions shall pertain only to the practical operation of stationary steam boilers and steam pumps. If the applicant is found proficient in said subjects, a license shall be granted him to have charge of and to operate stationary steam boilers of more than thirty horsepower. Such license shall continue in force for one year from the date the same is issued, and upon application to the district examiner may be renewed annually without being required to submit to another examination. The district examiner may, on written charges, after notice and hearing, revoke the license of any person guilty of fraud in passing the examination, or who, for any cause has become unfit to operate or have charge of stationary steam boilers. Any person dissatisfied with the action of any district examiner in refusing or revoking a license or renewal thereof, may appeal in accordance with sections 119.01 to 119.13, inclusive, of the Revised Code.

SECTION 4739.13 (1058-1a). APPLICATION FOR LICENSE TO OPERATE STATIONARY STEAM BOILERS; EXAMINATION; LICENSE; RENEWAL; REVOCATION; APPEAL

Any person who desires to operate or have charge of a stationary steam boiler of more than thirty horsepower, carrying a pressure of no more than fifteen pounds per square inch, except a person licensed under section 4739.05 or 4739.12 of the Revised Code, shall make application to the district examiner of steam engineers for a license upon a blank furnished by the examiner, and shall pass an examination on the construction and operation of steam boilers and appurtenances, under such rules and regulations as may be adopted by the chief examiner of steam engineers, which rules and regulations and standards of examination shall be uniform throughout the state and shall be in accordance with sections 119.01 to 119.13, inclusive, of the Revised Code. Examination questions shall pertain only to the practical operation of stationary steam boilers carrying less than fifteen pounds of pressure and appurtenances.

If the applicant is found proficient in said subjects a license shall be granted him to have charge of and to operate stationary steam boilers of more than thirty horsepower and operating at less than fifteen pounds pressure. Such license shall continue in force for one year from the date the same is issued, and renewed annually without the holder being required to submit to another examination. The district examiner may, on written charges, after notice and hearing, revoke the license of any person guilty of fraud in passing the examination, or who, for any cause has become unfit to operate or have charge of stationary steam boilers. Any person dissatisfied with the action of any district examiner in refusing or revoking a license or renewal thereof, may appeal to the chief examiner who shall review the proceedings of the district examiner and decide the merits of the appeal.

SECTION 4739.14 (1058-1b). FEES

The fee for examination of applicants for licenses under Section 4739.01 to 4739.15, inclusive, of the Revised Code, shall be fifteen dollars to be paid at the time of examination. The fee for each original or renewal of a license issued under section 4739.01 to 4739.15, inclusive, of the Revised Code, shall be fifteen dollars. Upon renewal, the licensee shall be furnished a certificate of renewal. All fees provided for in this section shall be paid by cash, money order, or certified check, to the division of examiner of steam engineers which shall transmit the same to the treasurer of state to the credit of the general revenue fund.

(Effective December 11, 1967)

SECTION 4739.15 (1058-1c). PROHIBITION

No owner, user, or person in charge of a stationary steam boiler shall violate sections 4739.11 to 4739.15, inclusive, of the Revised Code.

Penalty, 4739.99 (B)

SECTION 4739.99 PENALTIES

(A) Whoever violates section 4739.08 of the Revised Code shall be fined not to exceed five dollars.
(B) Whoever violates section 4739.09 or 4739.15 of the Revised Code shall be fined not less than ten or more than one hundred dollars.

RULES AND REGULATIONS GOVERNING THE EXAMINATION AND LICENSING OF APPLICANTS FOR STATIONARY STEAM ENGINEERS', BOILER OPERATORS' AND LOW PRESSURE BOILER OPERATORS' LICENSES

Effective January 1, 1977

EXAMINATIONS EVERY WEEK, BEGINNING AT 8:00 A.M. ON A DAY ESTABLISHED BY APPOINTMENT.

THE FOLLOWING UNIFORM RULES AND REGULATIONS GOVERNING EXAMINATIONS FOR STATIONARY STEAM EN-GINEERS, BOILER OPERATORS, AND LOW PRESSURE BOILER OPERATORS LICENSES ARE PURSUANT TO LAW:

4101:11-1-01. APPLICATIONS

(A) Examinations shall be given by appointment only and each applicant's request for examination must be received fourteen days prior to taking such examination. Each initial request shall be accompanied by a certified statement of experience on the form provided by the division of steam engineers. In lieu of this form, a license from another state or political subdivision thereof, marine license or a D.D. 214 will be accepted with proper classification and service time.

(B) If the request for examinations is approved the applicant will be examined within sixty days of date request is received. The applicant will be notified at least five days prior to assigned examination date, and a copy of such notice sent to the chief of examiners of steam engineers.

(C) Each applicant shall furnish two personal facial photographs taken not more than six months prior to the date of the applicant's examination; one to be attached to the application at the time of examination; the second to be attached to the original license when issued.

(D) An applicant when appearing for the examination shall make application in ink on a blank furnished by the examiner and shall make affidavit attesting that each and every statement in this application is true and shall acknowledge that any false statement included therein constitutes grounds for revocation of license.

(E) An applicant may be examined in a district other than that in which the applicant is employed or resides, provided the applicant secures from the chief examiner of steam engineers permission to take such examination.

4101:11-1-02. EXPERIENCE FOR LOW-PRESSURE BOILER OPERATORS

No person shall be permitted to take an examination for low-pressure boiler operator's license, unless:

(A) The applicant has reached the age of eighteen years.
(B) The applicant must have one of the following experience qualifications:
   (1) 600 hours practical experience as a steam engineer, oiler, boiler operator, boiler operator's helper, or boiler repair person experienced with duties that pertain to steam boiler operation.
   (2) 300 hours practical experience as a steam engineer, oiler, boiler operator, boiler operator's helper, or boiler repair person experienced with duties that pertain to steam boiler operation and 300 hours of boiler construction and/or boiler maintenance experience.
   (3) 300 hours practical experience as a steam engineer, oiler, boiler operator, boiler operator's helper, or boiler repair person experienced with duties that pertain to steam boiler operation and the successful completion of a thirty-six hour course in an approved program teaching steam boiler operation and boiler maintenance.

4101:11-1-03. EXPERIENCE FOR HIGH-PRESSURE BOILER OPERATORS

No Person shall be permitted to take an examination for high-pressure boiler operator's license, unless:
(A) The applicant has reached the age of eighteen years.
(B) The applicant must have one of the following experience qualifications:

(1) 1200 hours practical experience as a steam engineer, oiler, boiler operator, boiler operator's helper, or boiler repair person experienced with duties that pertain to steam boiler operation.

(2) 600 hours practical experience as a steam engineer, oiler, boiler operator, boiler operator's helper or boiler repair person experienced with duties that pertain to steam boiler operation and 600 hours of boiler construction and/or boiler maintenance experience.

(3) 600 hours practical experience as a steam engineer, oiler, boiler operator, boiler operator's helper, or boiler repair person experienced with duties that pertain to steam boiler operation and the successful completion of a sixty-hour course in an approved program teaching steam boiler operation and boiler maintenance.

4101:11-1-04. EXPERIENCE FOR STATIONARY STEAM ENGINEERS

No person shall be permitted to take an examination for stationary steam engineer's license, unless:

(A) The applicant has reached the age of eighteen years.

(B) The applicant must have one of the following experience qualifications:

(1) 1800 hours practical experience as a steam engineer, oiler, boiler operator, boiler operator's helper, or boiler repair person experienced with duties that pertain to the operation of steam reciprocating engine, turbine or boiler

(2) 900 hours practical experience as a steam engineer, oiler, boiler operator, boiler operator's helper, or boiler repair person experienced with duties that pertain to the operation of steam reciprocating engine, turbine or boiler and 900 hours of steam engine, turbine or boiler construction and/or maintenance experience.

(3) 900 hours practical experience as a steam engineer, oiler, boiler operator, boiler operator's helper, or boiler repair person experienced with duties that pertain to the operation of steam reciprocating engine, turbine or boiler and the successful completion of a ninety-six hour course in an

approved program teaching steam engineering and power plant maintenance

4101:11-1-05. EXPERIENCE AND APPROVED COURSE

(A) The experience for all examinations in rules 4101:11-1-02, 03 and 04 must be obtained on equipment with a manufacturer's rating of at least thirty horsepower.
(B) An approved course shall be a course approved by the state board of education, division of vocational education.
(C) The curriculum of the course and the instructor shall meet minimum requirements of the state board of education, division of vocational education.
(D) The request for approval of the course or instructor must be by written application, to the state board of education, division of vocational education, stating course curriculum, and instructor's qualification.

4101:11-1-06. FEE

The application for examination under rules 4101:11-1-02, 03 and 04 must be accompanied by the fee required by section 4739.14 of the Revised Code (regardless of the applicants' success or failure on examination, this fee is non-refundable).

4101:11-1-07. GRADE REQUIRED TO QUALIFY FOR LICENSES

Except as provided in rule 4101:11-1-11, a license shall be issued within thirty days after the completion of the examination to any applicant who receives a score of at least seventy per cent on the questions submitted at the examination.

4101:11-1-08. EXAMINATION PROCEDURES

All examinations shall be in writing by the applicant and be in the English language.
(A) Applicants shall not be permitted to converse with other applicants during examination. No information references shall be used during an examination except those supplied by the chief examiner of steam engineers.

(B) Examiners of steam engineers may use the common slide valve engine and duplex pump models in examination at their home offices. If used, a record shall be made upon the application showing whether or not the applicant understands the principle of valve setting.

4101:11-1-09. SCOPE OF EXAMINATIONS

(A) The examination for engineer's license shall consist of a list of fifty practical questions on the construction and operation of stationary steam boilers and stationary steam engines, steam pumps, and on the subject of hydraulics.

(B) The examination for boiler operator's license shall consist of a list of forty practical questions on the construction and operation of stationary steam boilers, steam pumps, and hydraulics.

(C) The examination for a low-pressure boiler operator's license shall consist of a list of thirty practical questions pertaining to the operation of stationary steam boilers of less than fifteen pounds pressure and their appurtenances.

(D) An examiner shall not submit to an applicant for license any questions which have not been supplied by the chief examiner of steam engineers. The chief examiner of steam engineers shall with the assistance of others designated by the chief, review all test questions and update as needed every five years or less.

4101:11-1-10. METHOD OF GRADING ANSWERS TO EXAMINATION QUESTIONS

(A) Examination papers for engineer's license shall be graded on a basis of ten for a correctly answered question.
   (1) If the answer to any question is incomplete or partly correct, the examiner shall give credit as to the value of the answer.
   (2) All percentages allowed for correct answers shall be added and the total divided by five.

(B) Examination papers for boiler operator's license shall be graded on a basis of ten for a correctly answered question.
   (1) If the answer to any question is incomplete or partly correct, the examiner shall give credits as to the value of the answer.

(2) All percentages allowed for correct answers shall be added and the total divided by four.

(C) Examination papers for low-pressure boiler operator's license shall be graded on a basis of ten for a correctly answered question.

    (1) If the answer to any question is incomplete or partly correct, the examiner shall give credit as to the value of the answer.

    (2) All percentages allowed for correct answers shall be added and the total divided by three.

4101:11-1-11. CLASSIFICATION OF LICENSES

(A) A third-class engineer's license shall be granted to an applicant who qualifies for and submits to an engineer's examination and receives a percentage of seventy or more.

(B) A second-class engineer's license shall be granted to an applicant who qualifies for and submits to an engineer's examination and receives a percentage of seventy-five or more, provided such applicant has had 3600 hours practical experience as an actual operating stationary steam engineer.

(C) A first-class engineer's license shall be granted to an applicant who qualifies for and submits to an engineer's examination and receives a percentage of eighty-five or more, provided such applicant has had 5400 hours practical experience as an actual operating stationary steam engineer.

(D) A boiler operator's license shall be granted to an applicant who qualifies for and submits to a boiler operator's examination and receives a percentage of seventy or more.

(E) A low-pressure boiler operator's license shall be granted to an applicant who qualifies for and submits to a low-pressure boiler operator's examination and receives a percentage of seventy or more.

4101:11-1-12. RE-EXAMINATION OF APPLICANTS

Applicants who fail to pass an examination may request an appointment for re-examination in the manner provided in 4101:11-1-01, provided further that they must wait a period of twenty-five days from the date of their last examination before the applicant can be re-examined for the same class or higher class license. However, an applicant failing to pass an examination for a license may apply and be re-examined as soon thereafter as practical to obtain a lower class license.

4101:11-1-13. EXAMINATION FOR HIGHER CLASS LICENSE

(A) If a person holding an engineer's, boiler operator's, or low-pressure boiler operator's license takes an examination for the purpose of obtaining a higher grade license and fails to secure the required percentage, such failure shall in no way affect the license already held by such person, and such license holder may have the same renewed on or before the date of expiration.

(B) A person obtaining a higher class license must return any lower class license issued by division of steam engineers to the examiner before a higher class license may be issued.

4101:11-1-14. APPEALS

A person dissatisfied with the action of the examiner in refusing a license may appeal to the chief examiner of steam engineers within thirty days after the date of mailing notice of such refusal. The applicant shall also have the right to a hearing on such appeal as provided by the Administrative Procedure Act in sections 119.01 to 119.13 of the Revised Code.

4101:11-1-15. REVOCATIONS

(A) If after an examination, it develops that a license may have been obtained through fraud, such procedure may be followed as provided by Ohio laws in the revocation of license for cause.

(B) Provisions of Ohio laws pertaining to license revocation shall be followed in any action seeking to revoke the license of any person.

4101:11-1-16. LICENSE RENEWAL

(A) A license that is not renewed within sixty days after expiration, shall be expired permanently, unless good and sufficient reason is given for the failure to have it renewed with the time specified.

(B)   A license shall not be renewed without the renewal fee prescribed by section 4739.14 of the Revised Code. The renewal of a license shall be made through the examiner of the district in which the license holder is employed or resides, or the central office, if so notified.

4101:11-1-17. AFFIDAVIT FOR DUPLICATE LICENSE

If the license of an engineer, boiler operator, or low-pressure boiler operator should be lost, stolen, accidentally mutilated or destroyed, the licensed person shall make affidavit setting forth the facts in the case before obtaining a renewal or duplicate of the license. (Such affidavit may be made before a notary public or an examiner.) In lieu of the affidavit required by the rule, the examiner may accept any recognizable portion of the mutilated or destroyed license which shall be sufficient evidence for the renewal of the license. The examiner shall forward the affidavit or any evidence received to the chief examiner of steam engineers.

4101:11-1-18. NOTICE OF VIOLATION

If an owner, user, agent of any owner or user, or person in charge of a stationary steam engine of more than thirty horsepower, or stationary steam boiler of more than thirty horsepower violates any of the provisions of the law relating to the operation of such stationary steam engines or stationary steam boilers, written notice shall be given to the responsible party specifically stating the violation of law, and unless that person complies with the provisions of the law, proper legal procedure shall be executed.

4101:11-1-19. RULE FOR GIVING PUBLIC NOTICE

Prescribing the procedure of the chief examiner of steam engineers, department of industrial relations, state of Ohio, in giving public notice, as required by law, of intention to consider adopting, amending or rescinding a rule or regulation.

(A)   Public notice of hearings to be conducted by the chief examiner of steam engineers, department of industrial relations, to consider adopting, amending or rescinding a rule or regulation shall be advertised in five newspapers published in different counties and of general circulation in the state. At least thirty days' notice of the time and place of a public hearing shall be given by said notice which shall include a synopsis or the full text of the proposed rule, amendment, or rule to be rescinded, or a general statement of the subject matter to which such proposed rule relates, and the date, time, and place of the hearing on said proposed action.

(B) The chief examiner of steam engineers shall be authorized to give additional notice of such public hearing as the chief deems necessary; however, the giving of such additional notice shall not be mandatory, and the failure to give notice by any means other than as specified above in (A) shall not in any way invalidate any action which may be taken by the chief examiner of steam engineers.

Appendix B

MANAGEMENT ACTION PLAN; SHORT RANGE

Project Statement	Objective	Complete By
A. Establish a professional image within the dept.	1. To enhance communications between Plant Oper. & other departments	
	a) establish a dress code	10/30/87
	b) provide interdepartmental inservices	Ongoing
	c) accept chairmanship of safety committee	07/26/87
	2. To develop the competency level of the existing staff	
	a) provide formalized training	06/30/88
	b) provide in-house training	Ongoing
	c) provide cross-training of personnel	Ongoing
B. Cut back the department's work force size	1. Eliminate one full-time equivalent position	01/01/88
C. Completely reorganize the department structure and operating procedures	1. Restructure the Asst. Director's position as a working supervisor	08/01/87
	2. Reclassify department positions to separate personnel by level of competency	
	3. Monitor compliance of contracts affecting department operations	01/01/88
	4. Update all manuals in the dept. and develop a dept. S.O.P. manual	02/28/88

MANAGEMENT ACTION PLAN; SHORT RANGE (Cont'd)

Project Statement	Objective	Complete By
	5. Establish written routines for groundskeeping, snow removal, building maintenance . . . etc.	02/28/88
	6. Establish a manufacturer's blueprint file	Ongoing
	7. Eliminate weekend work schedules and job time punching	08/01/87
	8. Establish an eight-component work requisition system	10/30/87
	9. Institute in-house surveys, utility tracking, equipment life expectancies, building and grounds routines	12/30/87
	10. Establish communications between plant operations and administration	
	a) supply CEO with a monthly department activities report	08/01/87
	b) attend bi-weekly meetings with CEO	Ongoing
	c) copy CEO on all correspondence initiated from the department including meeting minutes	Ongoing
	11. Establish an emergency valve and switch list	03/01/88
	12. Write equipment start-up/shut-down procedures for posting	06/30/88
	13. Establish a parts and material inventory	01/01/88

MANAGEMENT ACTION PLAN; SHORT RANGE (Cont'd)

Project Statement	Objective	Complete By
D. Timely completion of projects having an Administration priority	1. CT scanner entrance and electrical circuit	07/15/87
	2. Human Services trailer completion	09/30/87
	3. Managers offices on second and third floor	09/30/87
	4. Improve landscaping	
	a) remove myrtle beds	11/30/87
	b) cut down dead trees	
	c) remove dead bushes	
	d) fill in bog areas	
	e) install walkway edging	
	5. Install handrails	03/30/88
	6. Balance air system	06/30/88
	7. Make determination of building settling problem	01/01/88

Appendix C

Budget year: 1986-87   Department: Plant Operations   Dept. No. 820

DESCRIPTION	TOTAL	INPUT CODE	JUL	AUG	SEPT	OCT	NOV	DEC	JAN	FEB	MARCH	APR	MAY	JUNE
(units of service)	1268856		105738	105738	105738	105738	105738	105738	105738	105738	105738	105738	105738	105738
(productive hours required)	(13684)		(1149)	(1149)	(1149)	(1130)	(1130)	(1136)	(1130)	(1136)	(1136)	(1136)	(1136)	(1149)
(total hours paid)	(15204)		(1377)	(1377)	(1377)	(1262)	(1262)	(1262)	(1262)	(1262)	(1262)	(1262)	(1262)	(1277)
EXPENSES:														
SALARIES AND WAGES	161466	820.000	13714	13714	13271	13714	13271	13714	13714	12384	13714	13271	13714	13271
PURCHASED SERVICES	4520	820.324	350	70	810	310	810	510	70	310	810	70	70	70
- lawn care	1600	.01			800						800			
- equipment evaluation	840	.02	70	70	70	70	70	70	70	70	70	70	70	70
- systems checks	600	.03				300				300				
- thermographic studies	500	.04					500							
- fire alarm monitoring	180	.05	180											
- fire extinguishers	300	.06					300							
- other	500	.07						500						

Prepared By: _____   Date: _____   Approved By: _____   Date: _____

141

Budget year: 1986-87   Department: Plant Operations   Dept. No. 820   Page 2 of 7

DESCRIPTION	TOTAL	INPUT CODE	JUL	AUG	SEPT	OCT	NOV	DEC	JAN	FEB	MARCH	APR	MAY	JUNE
DEPARTMENT SUPPLIES	39615	820.425	3315	3966	2100	3319	2145	3709	4465	2561	5181	2448	2518	3238
- electrical	2224	.01	1234	90	90	90	90	90	90	90	90	90	90	90
- light bulbs	783	.02		235		14					276	81		177
- HVAC/plumbing	7920	.03	660	660	660	660	660	660	660	660	660	660	660	660
- carpentry/construction	4236	.04	353	353	353	353	353	353	353	353	353	353	353	353
- building hardware	3552	.05	296	296	296	296	296	296	296	296	296	296	296	296
- preventive maintenance	3552	.06	46	46	46	46	46	46	1535	46	1557	46	46	46
- replacement parts	1260	.07	105	105	105	105	105	105	105	105	105	105	105	105
- water treatment	5932	.08	86	1349	73	902	312	395	1032	708	1052	519	105	551
- salts	4920	.09	366	366	366	366		1406			366		366	
- pesticides/herbicides	1176	.10	196	196	196	196							196	196
- other	2172	.11	181	181	181	181	181	181	181	181	181	181	181	181

Prepared By: _____   Date: _____   Approved By: _____   Date: _____

Budget year: 1986-87   Department: Plant Operations   Dept. No. 820   Page 3 of 7

DESCRIPTION	TOTAL	INPUT CODE	JUL	AUG	SEPT	OCT	NOV	DEC	JAN	FEB	MARCH	APR	MAY	JUNE
MINOR EQUIPMENT	1300	820.455	100	100	100	100	100	100	100	100	100	100	100	100
- pump/motor replacements	400	.01	100	100		100			100			100		
- system components	400	.02		100			100			100			100	
- other	400	.03			100			100			100			100
(UTILITIES EXPENSE)	264423		25444	25014	24803	21515	21010	20850	21069	20636	20163	20944	18433	20580
ELECTRICITY	148233	820.582	15862	14944	14833	12355	11313	9481	10360	8703	10351	13426	12942	13833
NATURAL GAS	86585	820.583	6491	7000	6854	7115	7446	9333	9536	10715	7602	7193	3239	4411
WATER	11912	820.584	1364	1232	1302	925	1005	873	788	757	837	945	981	993
FUEL OIL	1000	820.585										1000		
SEWAGE	16394	820.586			5389			3865						3981

Prepared By: _____   Date: _____   Approved By: _____   Date: _____

Physical Plant Operations Handbook

Budget year: 1986-87   Department: Plant Operations   Dept. No. 820

DESCRIPTION	TOTAL	INPUT CODE	JUL	AUG	SEPT	OCT	NOV	DEC	JAN	FEB	MARCH	APR	MAY	JUNE
REPAIRS AND MAINTENANCE	124780	820.650	1040	1040	1040	1040	1040	1040	1040	1040	1040	1040	1040	1040
- building structure		.01												
- power plant equipment		.02												
- systems repair		.03												
- grounds		.04												
- mechanical spaces		.05												
- shop/office area		.06												
- renovations		.07												
- other		.08												
PM CONTRACTS	47565	820.651	1231	9390	1231	1231	9390	1391	1231	9390	1230	1230	9390	1230
- clinical engineering	26030	.01		6507			6507			6508			6508	
- fire warning system	6608	.02		1652			1652			1652			1652	
- other	14747	.03	1231	1231	1231	1231	1231	1231	1231	1230	1230	1230	1230	1230

Prepared By: _____   Date: _____

Approved By: _____   Date: _____

Budget year: 1986-87   Department: Plant Operations   Dept. No. 820   Page 5 of 7

DESCRIPTION	TOTAL	INPUT CODE	JUL	AUG	SEPT	OCT	NOV	DEC	JAN	FEB	MARCH	APR	MAY	JUNE
TRUCK EXPENSE	530	820.652	20	20	20	230	30	40	40	40	30	20	20	20
PM ELEVATOR		820.654												
LEASE EQUIPMENT	500	820.670	250	250										
SUBSCRIPTIONS	1240	820.759	50	50	50	450	250	90	50	50	50	50	50	50
- periodicals	40	.01						40						
- technical books	600	.02	50	50	50	50	50	50	50	50	50	50	50	50
- code manuals	400	.03				400								
- update service	200	.04					200							
TRAVEL/ENTERTAINMENT	1870	820.766	10	360	10	360	10	360	10	360	10	360	10	10
- seminar attendance	1750	.01		350		350		350		350		350		
- errands	120	.02	10	10	10	10	10	10	10	10	10	10	10	10

Prepared By: _____   Date: _____   Approved By: _____   Date: _____

Budget year: 1986-87   Department: Plant Operations   Dept. No. 820   Page 6 of 7

DESCRIPTION	TOTAL	INPUT CODE	JUL	AUG	SEPT	OCT	NOV	DEC	JAN	FEB	MARCH	APR	MAY	JUNE
PROFESSIONAL DUES	200	820.776							200					
- A.S.H.E.	200	.01							200					
- other		.02												
PROFESSIONAL DEVELOPMENT	3,000	820.777	150	300	450	300	150	300	450	300	150	300	150	
- service schools	1500	.01		300		300		300		300		300		
- formal schooling	900	.02	150		150		150		150		150		150	
- seminars/conferences	600	.03			300				300					
- correspondence course		.04												
- other		.05												
MISCELLANEOUS EXPENSE	1,200	820.780	100	100	100	100	100	100	100	100	100	100	100	100

Prepared By: _____   Date: _____   Approved By: _____   Date: _____

Budget year: 1986-87   Department: Plant Operations   Dept. No. 820   Page 7 of 7

DESCRIPTION	TOTAL	INPUT CODE	JUL	AUG	SEPT	OCT	NOV	DEC	JAN	FEB	MARCH	APR	MAY	JUNE
LICENSES	338	820.858												
- boilers/pv		.01			288					50				
- elevator		.02			180					50				
- pickup truck		.03			168									
- other		.04												
BOILER & MACHINERY INSURANCE	3019	820.882				3019								

Prepared By: _____   Date: _____   Approved By: _____   Date: _____

Appendix D

RFQ FOR DEMOLITION CONTRACT

October 7, 1985

Dear   :

My corporation invites you to submit a bid for the demolition and removal of all buildings and structures which once comprised the   on our   property.

Attached is a request for quotation which spells out the project and proposal requirements.

In order to be considered for hire on the project, all submittals must adhere to the dictates of the request for quotation and be submitted in triplicate.

If you need additional information/clarification or want to make arrangements for inspecting the facility, please contact me at   Ext.

Sincerely,

Director, Plant Operations

KLP:shp
Encl.

SECTION I: BIDDING INFORMATION

A. INVITATION TO BID
   TO: Prospective Contractors
   FROM: My corporation
   SUBJECT: Request for quotation dated   , for demolition/removal of all out structures on the   property.

TIME: All bids must be received in the office of the Director of Plant Operations, by 2 P.M. on October 31, 1985. It is expected that the project will begin after December 1, 1985.

B. BIDDER INSTRUCTIONS

1. Bidders should carefully examine the specifications and fully inform themselves as to all conditions and matters which in any way may affect the work or cost thereof. Should a bidder find discrepancies or omissions in the specifications or other documents or should he be in doubt of their meaning, he should at once notify Mr.   at   and obtain clarification prior to submitting any bid.

2. All comments made pertaining to bid specifications shall be referred to by their outline prefixes and titles.

3. In their quotation narrative, the bidders must show:
   a. Proof of a certificate of indemnification for professional liability in the amount of   (   ) or the intent and ability to acquire it. Prior to implementing the agreement, insurance must be in force, naming the corporation as third party receiver and must include a hold harmless clause, covering claims against the corporation for omissions and commissions of the contractor that end in loss, damage, cost and expense to the corporation.
   b. Which codes will be adhered to in the performance of the agreement.

4. Sealed bids must be sent under separate cover, in triplicate, projecting cost breakdowns for varying types and lengths of contracts proposed. Proposed payment schedules must also be enclosed.

5. Technical proposals must be sent under separate cover, in triplicate, defining the services to be provided by the contractor, subject to the conditions as stated in the RFQ for furnishing services as described herein and must be submitted on the contractor's letterhead.

6. The name of the responsible party or contact that the corporate liaison will confer with in all contract matters must be stated.

C. REJECTION OF BIDS

The corporation reserves the right to accept or reject any bid or any item(s) of any bids.

SECTION II: GENERAL CONDITIONS

A. CONTRACTOR'S RESPONSIBILITIES
1. Project requirements
   a. The contractor will be responsible for furnishing all necessary labor, materials, equipment, supervision and insurance for the job.
   b. The contractor will be responsible for acquiring all necessary permits and assuring utility services have been shut off and dead ended prior to beginning work.

B. CHARACTER OF WORK
1. All work is expected to be completed in a timely fashion, by qualified personnel in accordance with the strict dictates of the agreement. Unsatisfactory work shall be corrected at no cost to the corporation.
2. The workers will conduct themselves in a professional manner.
3. The job foreman will maintain a close rapport with the Director of Plant Operations and his Maintenance Supervisor, keeping them apprised of the status of the work on an ongoing basis.

C. ON-SITE WORK
1. The contractor will provide all necessary tools and equipment needed by the workers for proper performance of their work.
2. The workers are responsible for clean up of their work area prior to leaving the premises.

D. SUBCONTRACTORS
1. The corporation reserves the right to approve the use of any subcontractor.
2. The contractor shall provide the corporation with references on any subcontractor prior to submission for approval.

E. STANDARDS
   1. All work will be done in accordance with generally accepted criteria, engineering techniques and documentation procedures of the industry.
   2. Standards shall be consistent with Federal, State and local regulations, and shall reflect current engineering practices and other relevant voluntary, professional and official organizations and agencies.

F. PERSONNEL
   1. Qualifications.
      All workers on the project shall be qualified for the work they are charged with performing.

G. WORK SCHEDULE
   1. All work is to be performed during the daylight hours and scheduled in such a way as to limit the amount of noise made in the early morning hours.

H. INSPECTIONS
   1. Inspections of the facility prior to bid submission shall be coordinated with the corporate Director of Plant Operations.
   2. Frequent work progress inspections will be made jointly by the corporate representative and the contractor.

I. WORKMANSHIP
   1. Recourse for bad workmanship must be spelled out in the main body of the contract.

J. REFERENCES
   A minimum of three references must be given where the contractor has provided services similar to the size and scope of the agreement being quoted.

K. MEETINGS
   Frequent meetings must be held between the contractor's representative and the corporate Director of Plant Operations to review the progress of the work and resolve any problems associated with it.

L. COSTS

A complete list of the costs covering all areas must be submitted with the quotation.

SECTION III: PROJECT DESCRIPTION

A. Complete removal of all buildings, structures, floors and foundations, including:
   1. the main building, garage and connecting tunnel
   2. the barn, annex and pool building
   3. all asphalt except for the parking lot (please submit a separate bid for its removal)

B. All holes are to be backfilled with clean fill according to local ordinances. (The dirt on the property can be used for backfill.) The existing contour of the property is to be maintained.

C. A drainage trench running alongside the parking lot will be re-trenched and kept clear of debris from the project.

SECTION IV: OTHER CONSIDERATIONS

A. The contractor will be responsible for keeping all roadways leading to and from the property clear of mud, debris and paper.

B. The property is to be rough graded at the completion of the project.

Appendix E

SAMPLE OUTLINE OF WORK REQUISITION SYSTEM

The Physical Plant Operations Department is abandoning the existing method used for requisitioning work in the building and is instituting a new WORK REQUISITION SYSTEM. Components of the system are:

1. WORK REQUISITION FORMS
2. WORK REQUISITION LOG
3. MONTHLY COST CENTER CHARGE LOG
4. STATION REPAIR FORMS
5. MAINTENANCE ROUNDS (CART)
6. WORK REQUISITION DISTRIBUTION SHEET
7. PROJECT WORK SHEET

The following lists each of the components, stating their intended use and advantage over the present system:

1. WORK REQUISITIONS (Form No. 1)
   Intended use:
   The new WORK REQUISITION FORMS are multi-copy, carbon-loaded, sequentially numbered sheets which are to be used by Department Heads for communicating the need for services to be provided by the Physical Plant Operations Department. Any department in the building may use this form to request work to be performed that is not of a routine or emergency nature. Routine maintenance is uncomplicated work requiring little time and/or materials which generally can be handled on the spot by maintenance personnel . . . i.e., torn carpet repair, burned out light bulbs, minor adjustments, oiling, small leaks . . . etc.

Routine maintenance will be performed by the maintenance rounds-man, due to his findings during his tour or as the result of notations made on the Station Repair Form by personnel in that area. As always, EMERGENCY ONLY situations will continue to be handled

by telephoning the Physical Plant Operations Department at extensions   and   or the Director of Physical Plant Operations
at extension

PROCEDURES FOR USE:
With the installation of any system of this complexity comes certain
guidelines that must be strictly adhered to, if it is to be implemented
successfully. In order for all cost centers using the new form to
derive the benefits built into it, the upper portion of the FORM must
be completely filled out by the requisitioner, his/her cost center
number entered into the appropriate space and all FORMS must be
signed by the Department Head.

After filling in the WORK REQUISITION, the department head
should retain the pink copy for his/her follow-up and either send
the other three copies to the Director of Physical Plant Operations
or give them to the maintenance roundsman who will make certain
that he receives them.

In the event that a WORK REQUISITION is either disapproved or
the job deferred to a later date, the department head will receive a
copy of the original WORK REQUISITION FORM from the Director
of Physical Plant Operations, stating the reason for the disapproval
or deferment. This copy should be matched to the file copy he/she
retained for follow-up. In any case, the Director of Physical Plant
Operations will maintain contact with the originator of the WORK
REQUISITION until such time as a conclusion is drawn concerning
the work requested.

SPECIFIC:
Every maintenance repair request not deemed routine in nature
will prompt the use of a WORK REQUISITION. The Director
of Physical Plant Operations will place all pertinent information on a
WORK REQUISITION form when an EMERGENCY work request
is made via the telephone. Upon receipt of any WORK REQUISI-
TION, an entry will be made in the WORK REQUISITION LOG
enabling monitoring of the work through final disposition of the
FORM.

Each FORM will contain information reflecting the cost of material
and labor time that was needed to complete the work requested. This
information will be entered onto the FORM by the assigned worker.

The Physical Plant Operations Department will keep one copy of the FORM in its permanent files. A second copy will be given to the appropriate maintenance person/persons who will do the actual work. After the assigned task is completed, the assignee will fill in his/her portion of the FORM and return it to the Physical Plant Operations Office for recording. Once the final log entry has been made, a completed copy of the WORK REQUISITION, showing spent time and material costs, will be forwarded to the originator for his/her records.

ADVANTAGES:
a. provides for follow-up of uncompleted or deferred work by the initiator of the WORK REQUISITION
b. improves communications between department heads and the Physical Plant Operations Department
c. allows for planning and prioritization of projects
d. enables daily monitoring of work performance and backlogs
e. ensures that the right person is assigned to each task
f. lends itself to cost effective, bulk purchasing of materials
g. makes use of a maintenance cart and the STATION REPAIR FORM
h. provides better overall response to individual department's repair needs
i. uncovers nuisance trouble spots
j. improves quality control

RESPONSIBILITY:
The Director of Physical Plant Operations is responsible to ensure this procedure is implemented and carried out.

AUTHORITY:
The authority to change this policy lies with the Director of Physical Plant Operations.

RECISIONS:
This action rescinds all previous policies concerning the subject.

2. WORK REQUISITION LOG (Form No. 2)
   Intended use:

The WORK REQUISITION LOG is a permanent record maintained by the Physical Plant Operations Department that enables constant monitoring of individual WORK REQUISITION status.

ADVANTAGES:
  a. tells who the WORK REQUISITION was assigned to
  b. allows prioritization of work
  c. doubles as a work backlog summary
  d. provides maintenance repair cost information for tabulation of charges by cost center number
  e. improves quality control

3. MONTHLY COST CENTER CHARGE LOG (Form No. 3)
    Intended use:
The MONTHLY COST CENTER CHARGE LOG is a permanent record maintained by the Physical Plant Operations Department, that breaks down the costs of man-hour and material expenditures for repairs or alterations made within a cost center area, by maintenance personnel, as to the type of work performed, on a monthly basis.

ADVANTAGES:
  a. enables the Physical Plant Operations Department to forecast future staffing requirements
  b. makes historical information available to department heads when budgeting for future repair expenditures
  c. provides an accurate accounting, by cost center, of man-hour and material costs for annual summation and administrative forecasting and decision making
  d. improves quality control

4. STATION REPAIR FORMS (Form No. 4)
    Intended use:
The purpose of the STATION REPAIR FORM is to communicate the need for routine maintenance, in any given area of the building, to the maintenance roundsman. Anyone in the building may use this FORM to convey the information to him.

The FORM will be mounted on a clipboard and placed in a strategic place on each floor of the facility, providing access to anyone requiring routine maintenance work to be done.

Each day, as the roundsman makes his tour of the building he will review the FORM, floor by floor, and take care of any requested repairs dictated by it, along with his other duties.

ADVANTAGES:
    a. improves communication between the Physical Plant Operations Department and other departments
    b. assures that routine maintenance work is accomplished in a timely manner
    c. eliminates unnecessary and frequent telephoning of the Physical Plant Operations Department and maintenance personnel
    d. provides better tenant care by making maintenance personnel more aware of problems in their areas
    e. improves quality control

5. MAINTENANCE ROUNDS
Intended use:

In conjunction with the use of the STATION REPAIR FORMS, a MAINTENANCE ROUNDS schedule will be incorporated. During normal working hours, Monday through Friday, a maintenance man will be scheduled full-time, to completely tour the building in search of routine maintenance work. He will be responsible for checking all of the STATION REPAIR CLIPBOARDS and assuring that all work listed on them is done. He will make his rounds equipped with a MAINTENANCE CART on which will be available to him the tools, parts, or materials he needs to accomplish routine maintenance tasks.

ADVANTAGES:
    a. provides better visibility of maintenance personnel throughout the building
    b. assures timely routine maintenance repairs
    c. anticipates problems of a preventive nature
    d. improves communication between Physical Plant Operations and other departments

    e. eliminates wasteful back and forth travel by maintenance personnel for ladders, light bulbs, parts . . . etc.

    f. eliminates the need for frequent paging and telephoning of the Physical Plant Operations Department

    g. improves quality control

6. WORK REQUISITION DISTRIBUTION FORM (Form No. 5)

Intended use:

The WORK REQUISITION FORM is a tally sheet which enables the Physical Plant Operations Department to keep track of block allotments of WORK REQUISITIONS to individual cost centers.

ADVANTAGES:

    a. allows monitoring of and control over the distribution of WORK REQUISITION FORMS by cost center

    b. saves on the cost and waste of printed forms

    c. anticipates replenishment needs for the FORM   by cost center

    d. improves quality control

7. PROJECT SHEET (Form No. 6)

Intended use:

Once a WORK REQUISITION is approved, attached to it will be a PROJECT SHEET, wherein all components of the project are broken out. The estimated costs for materials, man hours to complete the project; whether or not the work will be contracted for or done in-house; expected starting and completion dates . . . etc., will all be reflected in this document.

ADVANTAGES:

    a. assures cost effective use of manpower and material resources

    b. dictates use of appropriate personnel for the job

    c. allows for prioritization of projects

    d. enables planning and scheduling of funds

    e. involves department heads in projects within their own areas

    f. improves quality control

(Form 1) MAINTENANCE WORK REQUISITION

DATE: DEPT.:   LOC: CC #

DESCRIPTION OF WORK NEEDED:

(CHECK ONE)

MAINT.

OTHER

DEPARTMENT HEAD SIGNATURE:

URG ☐   ROUT ☐   DEF ☐

FOR PLANT OPERATIONS DEPT. USE ONLY

DATE RECEIVED		APPROVED	
ASSIGNED TO		NOT APPROVED	
ASSIGNED BY		REASON:	
DATE ASSIGNED			

MAINTENANCE TYPE		ACTUAL COST	
CORRECTIVE		LABOR – $	
PREVENTIVE		MATERIAL – $	
ADM. APPROVAL		TOTAL – $	

JOB ESTIMATE	
MH	MAT

MATERIALS USED

COMPLETED	
DATE	BY
TIME SPENT	
REMARKS:	

PLANT COPY

(Form 2) WORK REQUISITION LOG

NO.	CC	REC	COMP	MH	MAT	ASGN	REMARKS

(Form 3) MONTHLY COST CENTER CHARGE LOG

| DEPARTMENT | CC | EQUIPMENT | | MAINTENANCE | | HVAC | RENOVATIONS | | TOTAL |
		REP	PM	REP	PM		LABOR	MAT	

(Form 4) STATION REPAIR FORM

AREA : ------------------

ASSIGNEE : ------------------

DESCRIPTION	DATE	LOCATION	NAME	COMP	INTL	COMMENTS

(Form 5) WORK REQUISITION DISTRIBUTION SHEET

DEPARTMENT	CC	ISSUE NOS.	ISSUE NOS.	ISSUE NOS.	ISSUE NOS.

(Form 6) PROJECT WORK SHEET

```
 PROJECT NO.   _____              DATE    _____
                                        MAN HOUR ESTIMATE
   COST ESTIMATE


   HOUSE LABOR        _____       _____
   HOUSE MATERIALS  _____         _____
   CONTRACTOR         _____        _____
                      _____        _____
                      _____        _____
   EQUIPMENT          _____        _____
                      _____        _____
                      _____        _____
   MISCELLANEOUS    _____          _____

   TOTAL              _____
                                        TOTAL MAN HOURS  _____


   CLARIFICATION :
   _____
   _____
   _____
   _____
   _____


   ACTUAL COSTS                            APPROVALS


   HOUSE LABOR        _____
   HOUSE MATERIALS  _____             YES   NO   DATE
   CONTRACTS          _____     DEPT HEAD
   EQUIPMENT          _____     PHYS PLT
   MISCELLANEOUS    _____       CONTROLLER
                                           ADMIN
       TOTAL          _____

                                           APPROVED        N/A
   DEVIATION          _____
```

Appendix F

SIX MONTH DEPARTMENT ASSESSMENT

TABLE OF CONTENTS

preamble

Prior to the installation of a new director, on June 11, 1984, the Plant Operations Department, then entitled Physical Plant Services, never established the formal structuring on programs necessary for its proper functioning as a viable entity within the organization.

Since the inception of operations in the new facility, in 1981, the parade of managers, in the director's position, has promoted development of poor interdepartmental communications and relationships, deterioration of morale within the department, projection of a less than professional image and gradual decline of the physical plant.

The honeymoon period, inherent to new institutions, is over. After three years in operation, jurisdictional agencies feel that sufficient time has elapsed to expect the programs they require installed, to be in place. The bugs should be out of the systems and an adequate preventive maintenance program well under way. The operating procedures within the department should be strictly defined and self perpetuating.

Such is not the case here. Many programs still need implemented, a formalized preventive maintenance program does not exist and departmental policies either still need written or are under revision.

The capacity for resolving these long-standing problems exists within the department itself. This document reflects the department's shortcomings and stipulates the course of action that will be taken in their correction.

i

introduction

A prior assessment of the department was made in June of 1983 by an outside agency. The citations in his report revolved around three major issues . . . i.e.,:

1) the lack of a proper work order system

2) poor maintenance and improper use of the emergency diesel generator

3) lack of PM on equipment

. . . the first and second issues have been addressed; the third issue will require a time commitment and monetary outlay, to be discussed later herein.

The remainder of the report is cursory, as concerns physical plant equipment problems and management observations.

This report will lend itself to a more in-depth assessment of the problems suffered by the department and will provide a time table for their resolution.

I. OBJECTIVE

Purpose

To appraise the effectiveness of the department in meeting the needs of the organization

Intent

To establish a basis for future planning within the department.

Scope

a) Evaluation of the department's operating efficiency.

b) Identification of potential areas for improvement.

c) Assessment of the needs of the department.

d) Indication of the department's future direction.

II. SUBSTRATUM

A. Department Management

Overview

In the six (6) months since June of 1984, the department has made significant progress in establishing itself as a working cog in the corporate apparatus.

Strides have been made in improving interdepartmental communications and creating a professional image of the department's operations and personnel.

A service attitude is evident in the department and morale has improved, as reflected in the individual pursuits of excellence witnessed of the workers in the day-to-day performance of their assigned tasks.

1

These and other accomplishments, noted later herein were made possible by the hands-off approach taken by administration, entrusting the entire operation of the department with its director.

1. Personnel

    a) staffing

        observation

        The existing staffing level is inadequate to maintain proper operations within the department.

        specific

        i)   The present 16 FTE's include 3.4 FTE's allocated to administrative and supervisory duties and ignores nonproductive time integral to the department. The average effective productive staff available is 9.2 FTE's.

        ii) The original staffing level was based on 199,620 square feet instead of the 228,738 square feet now used for computations and the outbuildings serviced were not included in the workup.

        iii) A minimum staffing level of 8 FTE's is required for preventive maintenance on and operation and repair of the physical plant equipment.

        conclusion

        The department would be better served by the addition of 2 competent HVAC mechanics to care for the physical plant equipment corrective and preventive maintenance needs.

2

recommendation No. 1

Hire 2 journeymen-level mechanics specifically for equipment care & operation.

observation

Except for typing, there is no clerical assistance available to the department director.

specific

i) Monitoring and tabulating of the work requisition system is presently done by the maintenance supervisor and department director.

ii) Tracking down prices and availability of materials takes much of the supervisor's and director's time.

iii) Writing minutes and collating data take up much of the supervisor's and director's time as does monitoring the preventive maintenance program.

conclusion

The addition of a clerical aide would free the director and supervisor to better pursue the duties of their offices.

recommendation No. 2

Hire a clerical aide having a background in maintenance operations to assist plant operations management personnel.

3

b) competency and training

observation

The competency level of the maintenance section personnel, on the whole, is average and comparable to other facilities of similar size.

specific

i) It is accepted and generally true that through the combined talents of the group, most problems can and have been solved as they have arisen in the past, but there remains the need for fully qualified, individual mechanics to resolve problems on a per-man basis.

ii) Although the quantity of work performed has vastly improved over the past six (6) months, at times the quality of the finished product is less than desirable.

iii) Whereas work is ultimately accomplished through a trial and error process, based on actual on-the-job practical experience, there remain many gaps in the theory knowledge required to properly finish assigned tasks, which often causes the job to take longer to complete than necessary.

conclusion

Productivity and quality assurance would improve in direct proportion to the training afforded the department's personnel.

recommendation No. 3

Plans should be made to provide for formalized training of maintenance personnel in specialty areas.

4

recommendation No. 4

A program of in-service and on-the-job cross training between trades, within the department, should be established.

recommendation No. 5

Full advantage should be taken of manufacturers' service schools when available.

c. projects capability

observation

Given the proper guidance, the maintenance group is capable of handling the majority of building renovations and equipment installations required by the organization. Some changes would have to be made in the operation to accommodate this valuable resource.

specific

i)   The present method of ordering materials through the corporate purchasing arm is time consuming, antiquated and fraught with inadequacies, resulting in receipt of the wrong materials, poor lead times and untimely completion of projects.

ii) Not enough time is available under the present staffing quota for one-on-one supervision of tradesmen or cross training or personnel during project work.

iii) The in-house inventory of construction materials is practically non-existent.

5

conclusion

Use of department talent for training and materials procurement should be encouraged and utilized.

recommendation No. 6

A full line of construction materials should be available in inventory for routine work performed on a daily basis.

recommendation No. 7

The plant operations department should be given the responsibility for and control over purchasing of all materials it uses.

recommendation No. 8

A library of building and equipment maintenance manuals should be established to afford reference for the department personnel.

2. Operations

    a) corrective maintenance

observation

An effective, seven-component work requisition system has been established, is operational and a success.

specific

    i) Interdepartmental communications have been improved.

    ii) More timely completion of repair requests is evident.

    iii) A history of maintenance needs for budget forecasting by cost center has been established.

6

conclusion

Work requests are now properly categorized, prioritized, and processed to completion.

recommendation

*see recommendation No. 2

b) routines

observation

There are instituted daily routines as regards physical plant tours and duties but they are not yet formalized.

specific

i) Presently the duties are being assigned by the supervisor and performed as understood by the individual assigned.

ii) Inspections are prompted by a less-than-adequate system of scheduling.

iii) Records of duties performed are not well documented.

conclusion

Formalization of routines and inspections will standardize the duties of the department's personnel and provide better control of the operation by the director.

recommendation No. 9

The department director should establish written policies to cover all personnel duty routines.

7

c. casualty prevention

observation

Much has been accomplished in this area over the past six (6) months with these exceptions:

specific

i) Piped gas monitoring is presently done haphazardly by three different departments and no specific guidelines have been established to delineate the duties of each.

ii) Fire drills are not properly scheduled or documented.

iii) The general and electrical safety policies are vague at best.

conclusion

Those areas as specified above must be upgraded if we are to be truly prepared for emergency situations.

recommendation No. 10

Monitoring of the gases should be assigned to one responsible department head, although a second should be involved as a backup.

recommendation No. 11

Appropriate forms and schedules should be generated to ensure performance and documentation of fire drills.

8

recommendation No. 12

The general and electrical safety policies should be rewritten to provide more detail to the subjects.

d. materials acquisition

observation

The present inventory is inadequate for daily completion of assigned tasks.
Note * see II, A, 1, c, i

specific

i)   Often times special trips must be made by department personnel to the outside for materials needed for small jobs.

ii) The material presently on hand is insufficient in quantity to perform most routine tasks.

iii) The costs associated with our present purchasing system are prohibitive.

conclusion

The corporation would enjoy considerable savings by eliminating outside runs for insignificant amounts of materials.

recommendation No. 13

A secured stock room should be built to house a materials inventory to accomodate the repair needs of the organization.

9

recommendation No. 14

Materials should be purchased in bulk quantities to avail the corporation of inherent cost savings and eliminate problems of lead times.

e. Policies and procedures

observation

Most of the policies written by the prior directors are superfluous and lacking in content and direction.
Note * see II, A, 2, c, iii

specific

i)   The existing policies were written to appease the need for documentation by regulatory bodies and little thought was put into their construction.

ii) Much of the information found in the policies/procedures is not appropriate to the issues addressed.

iii) Some subjects were neglected that are required to be addressed by governing entities.

conclusion

A competent, well detailed, inventory of policies/procedures is needed in the department.

recommendation No. 15

The director should review and revise the existing department policies as needed.

10

recommendation No. 16

Policies/procedures should be written for all areas required but previously ignored.

3. Contracts

observation

Presently all contracts involving plant operations are monitored and negotiated by the Purchasing Department causing confusion over what services are purchased, their cost and necessity.

specific

i) The plant operations director has little or no control over what contracts are in force or the services they are to provide.

ii) Often times contracts are renewed without notification to the department director.

iii) The need for many of the contracts may be in question.

conclusion

Monitoring of outside contract compliance would be better handled under the direction of the Plant Operations Department.

recommendation No. 17

Negotiations and control over outside service contracts affecting the Plant Operations Department should revert to its director.

11

recommendation No. 18

Monitoring of contract compliance should be performed systematically by the department.

4. Communications

   observation

   The department has made good progress in this area
   through the institution of the following:

   specific

   i) Establishment of a structured work requisition system having accountability built into it.

   ii) Regular and frequent relevant discussions within
   and outside of the department.

   iii) Informative and pertinent correspondence to appropriate administrative staff members.

   conclusion

   The department is making in-roads into bettering their
   relationship with other departments resulting in peer
   acceptance.

   recommendation

   * None

B. Building and Grounds

   1. Existing Conditions

   observations

   Over the summer, the department has done extremely
   well in upgrading the aesthetic appearance of the grounds.

12

specific

i) The maintenance cart rounds used in conjunction with the work requisition system anticipate minor and routine repairs before they are called to the attention of the department.

ii) The department has gone a long way in improving care on the outside of the building.

iii) The pride acquired by departmental personnel in the work they do contributes to a more concerted effort in keeping the building not only functional, but pleasing to the eye.

conclusion

Properly equipped, motivated and staffed, the maintenance section is capable of maintaining the building in good repair.

recommendation No. 19

Annual rehire of a full-time temporary employee at minimum wage for the months April through October each year to assist with groundskeeping chores.

recommendation No. 20

Establish work lists from insights gained by inspections of corporate properties.

C. Plant Equipment and Systems

  1. Status

observation

The existing condition of the physical plant equipment and systems is passable due to its relative newness, but is in the beginning stages of deterioration.

specific

i) The aging of the equipment, due to normal wear and tear, necessitates extraordinary care, not needed to this point.

ii) The preventive maintenance done to the equipment to date only met the minimum requirements for care of the equipment and systems.

iii) Diagnostic procedures are not routinely performed to establish equipment and system care needs.

conclusion

More attention paid to this critical area will result in dividends such as extended equipment and system life expectancies, less downtime and fewer costly repairs.

recommendation No. 21

A formalized, detailed, preventive maintenance program should be established.

recommendation No. 22

A schedule of regular equipment tear-down inspections should be implemented.

recommendation No. 23

Suitable diagnostic equipment should be purchased for care of physical plant machinery and systems.

2. Preventive Maintenance

observation

The existing preventive maintenance schedules are inadequate to properly care for plant equipment and systems.

14

specific

i) There is no procedure to assign preventive maintenance duties by work order.

ii) No documentation is maintained on the cost or completion of the work that is done.

iii) Significant backlogs occur when maintenance section personnel are used in other areas which causes some PM work to be neglected.

conclusion

If a formalized preventive maintenance program is not established, the result will be extremely costly to the facility.

recommendation No. 24

A formalized PM work order system should be instituted using state of the art computer software.

3. Documentation

observation

There are many facets of the operation which are still not monitored through documentation.

specific

i) The manufacturers' equipment files are patchy at best

ii) Inspection reports and equipment readings are not properly monitored.

iii) Equipment operating instructions and procedures are not posted.

15

conclusion

Lack of essential documentation prevents the director from properly monitoring the department's operations, interferes with smooth running of the department and does not comply with regulatory body requirements.

recommendation No. 25

Establish a manufacturers' index file for trouble-shooting equipment repairs.

recommendation No. 26

Design forms for equipment checklisting of inspections and readings.

recommendation No. 27

Write equipment operating instructions and procedures and post them by the equipment.

recommendation No. 28

Implement a monthly cross checking system of program compliance and contract monitoring.

4. Spare Parts Inventory

observation

There is no inventory of spare parts for either routine or emergency repairs of equipment located within or outside of the department.

specific

i) No machine parts except those which came with the equipment or scavenged from older, obsolete equipment are inventoried.

16

ii) No spare motors for air handling equipment or circu-
lating/supply pumps are inventoried.

iii) No back-up safety relief valves, traps . . . etc. for the
hot water supply and steam systems are inventoried.

conclusion

As the physical plant begins deteriorating, the lack of
adequate spares of back-ups will cause increasing disrup-
tions to corporate operations.

recommendation No. 29

Selected components of equipment critical to corporate operations should be kept in stock for emergency
use.

III. TIMETABLE OF CORRECTIONS

No.   **Recommendation**

1   Hire 2 journeymen-level mechanics specifically for equipment care and operation.
(3 months)

2   Hire a clerical aide having a background in maintenance
operations to assist plant management personnel.
(5 months)

3   Plans should be made to provide formalized training of
maintenance personnel in specialty areas.
(3 months)

4   A program of in-service, on-the-job cross training between
trades, within the department, should be established.
(ongoing)

17

No.	Recommendation
5	Full advantage should be taken of manufacturers' service schools when available. (ongoing)
6	A full line of construction materials should be available, in inventory, for routine work performed on a daily basis. (3 months)
7	The plant operations department should be given the responsibility for the control over purchasing of materials it uses. (1 month)
8	A library of building and equipment maintenance manuals should be established to afford reference for the department personnel. (ongoing)
9	The department head should establish policies to cover all personnel duty routines. (2 months)
10	Monitoring of piped gases should be assigned to one responsible department head, although a second should be involved as a back-up. (1 month)
11	Appropriate forms and schedules should be generated to ensure performance and documentation of fire drills. (12 months)
12	The general and electrical safety policies should be rewritten to provide more detail of the subjects. (4 months)

18

No.   Recommendation

13   A secured stock room should be built to house a mater-
      ials inventory to accommodate the repair needs through-
      out the building.
      (2 months)

14   Materials should be purchased in bulk quantities to avail
      the corporation of inherent cost savings and eliminate
      problems of lead times.
      (2 months)

15   The director should review and revise the existing depart-
      ment policies as needed.
      (ongoing)

16   Policies/procedures should be written for all our areas
      required but previously ignored.
      (ongoing)

17   Negotiation and control over outside service contracts
      affecting the Plant Operations Department should revert
      to its director.
      (1 month)

18   Monitoring of contract compliance should be performed
      systematically by the department.
      (1 month)

19   Annual re-hire of a full-time temporary employee at
      minimum wage for the months April through October
      each year to assist with groundskeeping chores.
      (4 months)

No.	Recommendation
20	Establish work lists from insights gained by inspections of corporate properties. (ongoing)
21	A formalized, detailed, preventive maintenance program should be established. (6 months)
22	A schedule of regular equipment tear-down inspections should be implemented. (6 months)
23	Suitable diagnostic equipment should be purchased for care of physical plant machinery and systems. (3 months)
24	A computerized PM work order system should be instituted using state of the art software. (9 months)
25	Establish a manufacturers' index for trouble-shooting equipment repairs. (ongoing)
26	Design forms for equipment inspections and readings. (ongoing)
27	Write equipment operating instructions and procedures and post them by the equipment. (3 months)
28	Implement a monthly cross-checking system of program compliance and contract monitoring. (2 months)

20

No.   Recommendation

29   Selected components of equipment critical to corporate operations should be kept in stock for emergency use. (1 month)

IV.   ACCOMPLISHMENTS TO DATE

A. Department Operations
— reclassified personnel
— job descriptions/performance standards/job factoring
— work requisition system
— maintenance cart/rounds routine
— diesel fuel analysis & treatment
— fire drills caught up
— work shift changes
— department renovations
— updated manuals
   *   adm SPP
   *   personnel
   *   safety
   *   emergency generator operation
— in-service programs for other departments
— monthly department activity report

B. Policies/Procedures

ADM#	DEPT#	POLICY
	PO-001	Maintenance Cart Rounds Routine
	PO-002	Employee Orientation
SPP 2.61	PO-003	Scheduled Working Hours
SPP 2.43	PO-004	Work Requisition System
	PO-005	Winter Groundskeeping
SPP 2.62	PO-006	Emergency Generator Testing Schedule
	PO-007	Emergency Generator Testing Procedure

21

PO-008   Operating Instructions — Generator
PO-009   Preventive Maintenance — Generator
PO-010   Shop and Job Clean Up

C. Priority Projects
  - environmental services trailer
  - office renovations
  - telephone system repair
  - work backlogs
  - TV hook-ups for audio-visual department
  - yard work
    * bog areas filled and seeded
    * clean out field behind garages
    * catch basin — south entrance
    * handicap spaces
    * memorial park
    * lay out of running track

D. Statistics
  - 8,083 separate job tasks
  - 10 policies written
  - 62 meetings attended by the director
  - 79 correspondences from the director
  - 12 in-services held in the department
  - 4 in-services held outside of the department

E. Training
  - Inservices
    * telephone repair
    * emergency generator operation
    * boiler dismantling and operation
    * orientation

22

* boiler water testing
* work requisition system
* fire safety
* safety relief valves
* elevator egress
* policies/procedures
* fire alarm system

— On-the-job training
  * use of power hammer
  * television servicing
  * key set repairs
  * maintenance cart rounds
  * pressure vessel fit-ups
  * wall preparation and construction
  * employee safety

Schools — Pneumatics and Hydraulics

V. DIRECTORS COMMENTS

A. Summary

Although the department is understaffed, it is on track in meeting my expectations to date. Deferred work has been kept at a minimum and the only area suffering is preventive maintenance which has to be reworked as before stated.

The maintenance supervisor does an excellent job of keeping materials and tasks co-ordinated, even with our present inadequate system of procurement.

Morale within the department has taken a turn for the better, due to the service attitude which has been instilled in the men.

23

An open line of communication has been established between Plant Operations and other departments throughout the facility.

Training is the watchword. If the department is to progress beyond the point we have established, a concerted effort must bc made to provide for the development of our present staff both monetarily and mentorily.

B. Future Direction

Once the department is properly staffed, structured and organized, it will become a service entity above reproach, and a source of pride for the corporation.

It can then branch out to encompass other service areas, under the umbrella of a single service organization, within the facility, become self perpetuating and cost-effective.

24

Appendix G

TABLES

Table 1. COMPOSITION OF AIR

Nitrogen	78%
Oxygen	21%
Argon	0.96%
Carbon Dioxide & other gases	0.04%

Table 2. ATMOSPHERIC PRESSURE PER SQUARE INCH

Barometer (ins. of mercury)	Pressure (lbs. per sq. in.)
28.00	13.75
28.25	13.88
28.50	14.00
28.75	14.12
29.00	14.24
29.25	14.37
29.50	14.49
29.75	14.61
29.921	14.696
30.00	14.74
30.25	14.86
30.50	14.98
30.75	15.10
31.00	15.23

Table 3. APPROXIMATE AIR NEEDS OF PNEUMATIC TOOLS, CFM

Grinders, 6- and 8-in. diameter wheels 50
    2- and 2½-in. diameter wheels .14-20
File and burr machines 18
Rotary sanders, 9-in. diameter pads 55
Sand rammers and tampers:
    1 x 4-in. cylinder 25
    1¼ x 5-in. cylinder 28
    1½ x 6-in. cylinder 39
Chipping hammers. 10-13 lb 28-30
    2-4 lb 12
Nut setters to 5/16 in., 8 lb. 20
    ½ to ¾ in., 18 lb. 30
Paint spray 2-20
Plug Drills 40-50
Riveters, 3/32- to 1/8-in. rivets .12
Rivet busters 35-39
Steel drills, rotary motors;
    To ¼ in., weighting 1¼-4 lb. .18-20
    ¼ to 3/8 in., weighing 6-8 lb. .20-40
    ½ to ¾ in., weighing 9-14 lb. .70
    7/8 to 1 in., weighing 25 lb. 80
Wood borers to 1-in. diameter, weighing 14 lb. 40

Table 4. AVERAGE ABSOLUTE ATMOSPHERIC PRESSURE

Altitude in feet reference to sea level	Inches of Mercury (in. Hg)	Pounds per sq. in. absolute (psia)
− 1,000	31.00	15.2
− 500	30.50	15.0
sea level 0	29.92	14.7
+ 500	29.39	14.4
+ 1,000	28.87	14.2
+ 1,500	28.33	13.9
+ 2,000	27.82	13.7
+ 3,000	26.81	13.2
+ 4,000	25.85	12.7
+ 5,000	24.90	12.2
+ 6,000	23.98	11.7
+ 7,000	23.10	11.3
+ 8,000	22.22	10.8
+ 9,000	21.39	10.5
+ 10,000	20.58	10.1

Table 5. CONCRETE FOR WALLS

(Per 100 Square Feet Wall)

Thickness	Cubic Feet Required	Cubic Yards Required
4″	33.3	1.24
6″	50.0	1.85
8″	66.7	2.47
10″	83.3	3.09
12″	100.0	3.70

Table 6. EARTH EXCAVATION FACTORS

Depth	Cubic Yards per Square Foot
2″	.006
4″	.012
6″	.018
8″	.025
10″	.031
1′-0″	.037
1′-6″	.056
2′-0″	.074
2′-6″	.093
3′-0″	.111
3′-6″	.130
4′-0″	.148
4′-6″	.167
5′-0″	.185
5′-6″	.204
6′-0″	.222
6′-6″	.241
7′-0″	.259
7′-6″	.278
8′-0″	.296
8′-6″	.314
9′-0″	.332
9′-6″	.350
10′-0″	.369

Table 7. BUILDING DESIGN LOADS

Occupancy or Use	Live Load Lbs. per Sq. Ft.
Apartment houses:	
Private apartments	40
Public stairways.	100
Assembly halls:	
Fixed seats	60
Movable seats	100
Corridors, upper floors	100
Corridors:	
First Floor	100
Other floors, same as occupancy served except as indicated.	
Dining rooms, public	100
Dwellings.	40
Hospitals and asylums:	
Operating rooms	60
Private rooms	40
Wards.	40
Public space	80
Hotels:	
Guest Rooms.	40
Public Rooms	100
Loft buildings.	125
Schools:	
Classrooms	40
Corridors	100
Sidewalks	250
Stairways	100
Stores	125

Table 8. CONCRETE CURING METHODS

Method	Advantage	Disadvantage
Wetting	Excellent results if constantly kept wet	Difficult on vertical walls
Straw	Insulator in winter	Can dry out, blow away, or burn
Curing Compounds	Easy to apply Inexpensive	Sprayer needed Can allow concrete to get too hot
Waterproof Paper	Prevents drying	Cost can be excessive
Plastic Film	Absolutely watertight	Must be weighed down

Table 9. LUMBER SIZES IN INCHES

Nominal	Seasoned
1 x 4	¾ x 3½
1 x 6	¾ x 5½
1 x 8	¾ x 7¼
1 x 10	¾ x 9¼
1 x 12	¾ x 11¼
2 x 4	1½ x 3½
2 x 6	1½ x 5½
2 x 8	1½ x 7¼
2 x 10	1½ x 9¼
2 x 12	1½ x 11¼
4 x 4	3½ x 3½
4 x 6	3½ x 5½
4 x 8	3½ x 7¼
4 x 10	3½ x 9¼
4 x 12	3½ x 11¼

Table 10. APPLIANCE ENERGY REQUIREMENTS

Major Applicances	Annual kWh
Air-Conditioner (room) (Based on 1000 hours of operation per year. This figure will vary widely depending on geographic area and specific size of unit.	860
Clothes Dryer	993
Dishwasher (includinn energy used to heat water)	2,100
Dishwasher only	363
Freezer (16 cu. ft.)	1,190
Range with oven	700
with self-cleaning oven	730
Refrigerator (12 cu. ft.)	728
Refrigerator - frostless (12 cu. ft.)	1,217
Refrigerator/Freezer (12.5 cu. ft.)	1,500
Refrigerator/Freezer - frostless (17.5 cu. ft.)	2,250
Washing Machine - automatic (including energy used to heat water)	2,500
Washing Machine - non-automatic (including energy to heat water)	2,497
washing machine only	76
Water Heater	4,811

Kitchen Appliances	
Blender	15
Broiler	100
Carving Knife	8

Table 10. (Continued)

Kitchen Appliances	Annual kWh
Coffee Maker	140
Deep Fryer	83
Egg Cooker	14
Frying Pan	186
Hot Plate	90
Mixer	13
Oven, Microwave (only)	190
Roaster	205
Sandwich Grill	33
Toaster	39
Trash Compactor	50
Waffle Iron	22
Waste Disposer	30

Heating and Cooling

Air Cleaner	216
Electric Blanket	147
Dehumidifier	377
Fan (attic)	281
Fan (circulating)	43
Fan (rollaway)	138
Fan (window)	170
Heater (portable)	176
Humidifier	163

Laundry

Iron (hand)	144

Health and Beauty

Germicidal Lamp	141
Hair Dryer	14
Heat Lamp (infrared)	13
Shaver	1.8
Sun Lamp	16
Toothbrush	.5
Vibrator	2

Home Entertainment

Radio	86
Television	
Black and White	
Tube type	350
Solid State	120
Color	
Tube type	660
Solid State	440

Table 10. (Continued)

Housewares	Annual kWh
Clock	17
Floor Polisher.	15
Sewing Machine	11
Vacuum Cleaner	46

Table 11. ALTERNATING CURRENT CALCULATIONS

	Alternating Current	
To Calculate	Three-Phase	Single-Phase
Amperes when horse-power is known	$\dfrac{\text{H.P.} \times 746}{1.73 \times E \times \%\text{Eff} \times \text{P.F.}}$	$\dfrac{\text{H.P.} \times 746}{E \times \%\text{Eff} \times \text{P.F.}}$
Amperes when kilo-watts are known	$\dfrac{\text{K.W.} \times 1000}{1.73 \times E \times \text{P.F.}}$	$\dfrac{\text{K.W.} \times 1000}{E \times \text{P.F.}}$
Amperes when K.V.A. are known	$\dfrac{\text{K.V.A.} \times 1000}{1.73 \times E}$	$\dfrac{\text{K.V.A.} \times 1000}{E}$
Kilowatts	$\dfrac{I \times E \times 1.73 \times \text{P.F.}}{1000}$	$\dfrac{I \times E \times \text{P.F.}}{1000}$
K.V.A.	$\dfrac{I \times E \times 1.73}{1000}$	$\dfrac{I \times E}{1000}$
Horsepower (Output)	$\dfrac{I \times E \times 1.73 \times \% \text{ Eff} \times \text{P.F.}}{746}$	$\dfrac{I \times E \times \%\text{Eff} \times \text{P.F.}}{746}$

E = Volts. K.W. = Kilowatts. P.F. = Power Factor. I = Amperes
%Eff. = Percent Efficiency. K.V.A. = Kilowatt amperes. H.P. = Horsepower

Table 12. KILOWATT CONVERSION FACTORS

Kilowatt Conversion Factors

1 kilowatt	=	1.3415 horsepower
	=	738 ft lb per sec
	=	44,268 ft lb per min
	=	2,656,100 ft lb per hr
	=	56.9 Btu per min
	=	3,413 Btu per hr

Table 13. EFFECTS OF ELECTRICAL CURRENT ON HUMANS

Current Values	Effect
1 ma	Causes no sensation
1 to 8 ma	Sensation of shock. Not painful
8 to 15 ma	Painful shock
15 to 20 ma	Cannot let go
20 to 50 ma	Severe muscular contractions
100 to 200 ma	Ventricular fibrillation
200 & over ma	Severe burns. Severe muscular contractions

Table 14. GEOMETRIC FORMULAS

Circumference of a circle	$C = \pi d$
Length of an arc	$L = \dfrac{n}{360} \times \pi d$
Area of a rectangle	$A = LW$
Area of a square	$A = s^2$
Area of a triangle	$A = \frac{1}{2}bh$
Area of a trapezoid	$A = \frac{1}{2}h \, (b + b^1)$
Area of a circle	$A = .7854d^2$, or $\frac{1}{4}\pi d^2$
Area of a sector	$S = \dfrac{n}{360} \times .7854d^2$
Area of an ellipse	$A = .7854ab$
Area of the surface of a rectangular solid	$S = 2LW + 2LH \dagger 2WH$
Lateral area of a cylinder	$S = \pi dh$
Area of the surface of a sphere	$S = \pi d^2$
Volume of a rectangular solid	$V = LWH$
Volume of a cylinder	$V = .7854d^2 h$
Volume of a sphere	$V = .5236d^3$, or $1/6\pi d^3$
Volume of a cube	$V = e^3$

Table 15. HEAT EQUIVALENTS

1 Btu	= 252 calories
1 kilocalorie	= 1000 calories
1 Btu/lb.	= .55 kcal/kg
1 Btu/lb.	= 2.326 kj/kg
1 kcal/kg	= 1.8 Btu/lb
1 Btu/hr	= 0.2931 watts

Table 16. HEAT GENERATED BY APPLIANCES

General lights and heating	3.4 Btu/hr/watt
2650 watt toaster	9100 Btu/hr
5000 watt toaster	19,000 Btu/hr
Hair dryer	2000 Btu/hr
Motor less than 2 HP	3600 Btu/hr/HP
Motor over 3 HP	3000 Btu/hr/HP

Table 17. HEAT LOSS FROM HOT WATER PIPING

Inches	Bare	Insulated
½	65	22
¾	75	25
1	95	28
1¼	115	33
1½	130	36
2	160	42
2½	185	48
3	220	53
4	280	68

Table 18. SPECIFIC HEATS OF COMMON SUBSTANCES

Aluminum	.2143
Brine	.9400
Coal	.314
Copper	.0951
Ice	.5040
Petroleum	.5110
Water	1.0000
Wood	.3270

Table 19. HEAT CONTENT OF COMMON FUELS

Number 6 fuel oil	152,400 Btu per gallon
Number 2 fuel oil	139,600 Btu per gallon
Natural Gas	950 to 1150 Btu per cubic foot
Propane	91,500 Btu per gallon

STEAM

Table 20. STEAM PRESSURE TEMPERATURE RELATIONSHIP

Gage Psi	Sat Temp F
0	212
5	228
10	240
20	259
30	274
40	287
50	298
60	308
70	316
80	324
90	331
100	338

Table 21. STEAM TRAP SELECTION

CHARACTERISTIC	INVERTED BUCKET	THERMOSTATIC
Method of Operation	Intermittent	Intermittent
Steam Loss	None	None
Resistance to Wear	Excellent	Good
Corrosion Resistance	Excellent	Excellent
Resistance to Hydraulic Shock	Excellent	Poor
Vents Air and CO-2 at Steam Temperature	Yes	No
Ability to Vent Air at Very Low Pressure	Poor	Excellent
Ability to Handle Start-up Air Loads	Fair	Excellent
Operation Against Back Pressure	Excellent	Excellent
Resistance to Damage from Freezing	Poor	Excellent
Ability to Purge System	Excellent	Good
Ability to Operate on Very Light Loads	Good	Excellent
Responsiveness to Slugs of Condensate	Immediate	Delayed
Ability to Handle Dirt	Excellent	Fair
Comparative Physical Size	Large	Small

TEMPERATURE

Table 22. COLOR SCALE OF TEMPERATURE

Color	Temperature
Incipient red heat	900-1100
Dark red heat	1100-1500
Bright red heat	1500-1800
Yellowish red heat	1800-2200
Incipient white heat	2200-2600
White heat	2600-2900

Table 23. CENTIGRADE/FAHRENHEIT SCALE

°C	°F
−50	−58
−40	−40
−30	−22
−20	− 4
−10	14
0	32
10	50
20	68
30	86
40	104
50	122
60	140
70	158
80	176
90	194
100	212
110	230
120	248
130	266
140	284
150	302
160	320

Table 24. WATER EQUIVALENTS

U.S. Gallons	x 8.33	= Pounds
U.S. Gallons	x 0.13368	= Cu. Ft.
U.S. Gallons	x 231.00	= Cu. Ins.
U.S. Gallons	x 3.78	= Litres

Table 24. (Continued)

Cu. Ins. of Water (39.2°)	x 0.036130	= Pounds
Cu. Ins. of Water (39.2°)	x 0.004329	= U.S. Gals.
Cu. Ins. of Water (39.2°)	x 0.576384	= Ounces
Cu. Ft. of Water (39.2°)	x 62.427	= Pounds
Cu. Ft. of Water (39.2°)	x 7.48	= U.S. Gals.
Cu. Ft. of Water (39.2°)	x 0.028	= Tons
Pounds of Water	x 27.72	= Cu. Ins.
Pounds of Water	x 0.01602	= Cu. Ft.
Pounds of Water	x 0.12	= U.S. Gals.

Table 25. SUPPLY LINE SIZES FOR COMMON FIXTURES

Laundry Tubs. . . . . .½ inch
Drinking Fountains . . . . .3/8 inch
Showers. . . . . .½ inch
Water-Closet Tanks . . . . .3/8 inch
Water-Closets (with flush valves). . . . . . .1 inch
Kitchen Sinks. . . . . .½ inch
Commercial-Type Restaurant
    Scullery Sinks . . . . .½ inch

Table 26. PRESSURE OF WATER

One foot of water = 0.4335 psi
One psi = 2.31 foot of water

Feet Head	Pressure Psi
10	4.33
15	6.49
20	8.66
25	10.82
30	12.99
35	15.16
40	17.32
45	19.49
50	21.65
55	23.82
60	25.99
70	30.32
80	34.65
90	38.98
100	43.31
200	86.63
300	129.95
400	173.27

Table 27. WATER REQUIREMENTS OF COMMON FIXTURES

Fixture	Cold, GPM	Hot, GPM
Water-closet flush valve	45	0
Water-closet flush tank	10	0
Urinals, flush valve	30	0
Urinals, flush tank	10	0
Lavatories	3	3
Shower, 4-in. head	3	3
Shower, 6-in. head and larger	6	6
Baths, tub	5	5
Kitchen sink	4	4
Pantry sink	2	2
Slop sinks	6	6

Glossary

ABSOLUTE PRESSURE — atmospheric pressure added to gage pressure

ABSOLUTE TEMPERATURE — the theoretical temperature when all molecular motion of a substance stops. minus 460 degrees fahrenheit

ACCESS FLOORING — a raised floor consisting of removable panels under which ductwork, wiring and pipe runs are installed

ACOUSTICAL CEILING — a ceiling composed of tiles having sound absorbing properties

AIR CHANGES — the number of times in an hour that a volume of air filling a room is exchanged

ALGAE — a form of plant life which causes fouling in water system piping; especially in cooling towers

AMBIENT TEMPERATURE — the temperature of the air immediately surrounding a device

ANEMOMETER — an instrument used for measuring air velocity

A.S.T.M. — American Society for Testing and Materials

ASTRAGAL — a molding or strip used to cover the joint where two doors meet

ATMOSPHERIC PRESSURE — the weight of the atmosphere measured in pounds per square inch

ATOMIZATION — the process of reducing a liquid into a fine spray

AXIAL FAN — a device which discharges air parallel to the axis of its wheel

BACKWASH — the backflow of water through the resin bed of a water softener during the cleaning process

BEARING WALL — a wall structure which supports floors and roofs

BIOCIDE — a substance that is destructive to living organisms that is used in refrigeration systems by design

BLOWBACK — the difference in pressure between when a safety valve opens and closes

B.O.C.A. — Building Officials and Code Administrators International, Inc.

BOILER HORSEPOWER — the evaporation of 34.5 pounds of water per hour from a temperature of 212F into dry saturated steam

BOILING POINT — The temperature at which a liquid is converted to a vapor corresponding to its pressure

BOYLES LAW — a law of physics dealing with variations in gas volumes and pressures at constant temperatures

BRITISH THERMAL UNIT (BTU) — a unit measurement of heat. the amount of heat needed to raise the temperature of one pound of water, one degree Fahrenheit

BUILT UP ROOF — a roof membrane comprised of layers of asphalt-saturated felts laminated together with pitch

CAISSON — A concrete foundation support poured through inferior soil which rests on solid rock or good soil

CAPILLARY ACTION — the capacity of a liquid to be drawn into small spaces

CARRYOVER — a condition whereby water or chemical solids enter the discharge line of a steam boiler

CAVITATION — the formation of vapor pockets in a flowing liquid

CHIMNEY EFFECT — the tendency of air to rise within confined vertical passages when heated

COEFFICIENT OF HEAT TRANSMISSION (U) — the amount of heat measured in Btu's transmitted through materials over time. the heat transmitted in one hour per square foot per degree difference between the air inside and outside of a wall, floor or ceiling.

COEFFICIENT OF PERFORMANCE (COP) — the ratio of work performed to the energy used in performing it

COMBUSTION EFFICIENCY — the ratio of the heat released from a fuel as it burns, to its heat content

COMFORT ZONE — a range of temperature and humidity combinations within which the average adult feels comfortable

CONCENTRATIONS — the number of times that dissolved solids increase in a body of water as a one-to-one multiple of the original amount due to the evaporation process

CONDENSATION — the process of returning vapor back to its liquid state through the extraction of latent heat

CONTINGENCY PLANNING — a process which anticipates and prescribes corrective action to be taken in the event of unforeseen circumstances and emergency situations

CONTINUOUS BLOWDOWN — a process whereby solids concentrations within a body of water are controlled through the constant removal and replacement of the water

COUNTERFLASHING — a downward turned flashing which overlaps an upward turned flashing used for protecting against the entry of water into a structure

COUNTERFLOW — a method of heat exchange that brings the coldest portion of one moving fluid into contact with the warmest portion of another

C.P.U. — Central Processing Unit. the part of a computer wherein the arithmetic and logical functions are performed

CURING COMPOUND — a liquid which is sprayed onto new concrete to prevent premature dehydration

D.E.R. — Department of Environmental Resources

DAYLIGHTING — using naturally occurring light to illuminate the interiors of buildings

DEAERATION — the removal of entrained air from a liquid

DEGREE DAY — a unit representing one degree difference between indoor and average outdoor temperatures in a day

DEGREE OF SUPERHEAT — the difference between the saturation temperature of a vapor and its actual temperature at a given pressure

DESICCANT — a drying agent such as silica gel or activated alumina that is used to absorb and hold moisture

DEW POINT TEMPERATURE — the lowest temperature that air can be without its water vapor condensing

DRY BULB TEMPERATURE — the temperature of the air as measured on a thermometer

E.P.A. — Environmental Protection Agency

ECONOMIZER — a heat recovery device that utilizes waste heat for preheating fluids

E.D.P. — Electronic Date Processing

EFFLORESCENCE — chemical salt residue deposited on the face of masonry caused by the infiltration of water into a structure

ELECTROLYSIS — a chemical reaction between two substances prompted by the flow of electricity at their point of contact

ELECTROSTATIC PRECIPITATOR — an electrically charged device used for removing dust particles from an air stream

ENTRAINMENT — the inclusion of water or solids in steam, usually due to the violent action of the boiling process

EVAPORATION — the transformation of a liquid into its vapor state through the application of latent heat

EXCESS AIR — the air supplied for the combustion process in excess of that theoretically needed for complete oxidation

FEEDWATER TREATMENT — the conditioning of water with chemicals to establish wanted characteristics

FIRE SEPARATION WALL — a wall dividing two sections of a building used to prevent the spread of fire

FLAME SPREAD RATING — the measure of how fast fire will spread across the surface of a material once it is ignited.

GAGE PRESSURE — absolute pressure minus atmospheric pressure

GREENHOUSE EFFECT — the result of trapping radiant heat from the sun within an enclosure

HALOGENS — chlorine, iodine, bromine or fluorine

HALIDE TORCH — a device which uses an open flame for detecting refrigerant leaks

HARDNESS — a term used to describe the calcium and magnesium content of water

HEATING SURFACE — that portion of a heat exchange device which is exposed to the heat source and transfers heat to the heated medium

HERMETIC COMPRESSOR — a unit wherein a compressor and its driving motor are contained in a single, sealed housing

HUMIDISTAT — a control device which responds to changes in the humidity of air

HYDROSTATIC TEST — a procedure in which water is used to determine the integrity of pressure vessels

HYDRONIC HEATING SYSTEM — a heating system wherein hot water is circulated through convectors

ION EXCHANGE — a process for removing impurities from water on the atomic level through the selective repositioning of electrons.

KELVIN SCALE — a temperature scale incremented in centigrade that begins at absolute zero (−273C)

LATENT HEAT OF CONDENSATION — the heat extracted from a vapor in changing it to a liquid with no change in temperature

LATENT HEAT OF EVAPORATION — the heat added to a lquid in changing it to a vapor with no change in temperature

LATENT HEAT OF FUSION — the heat added to a solid in changing it to a liquid with no change in temperature

LIGHTNING ARRESTER — a device located in an electrical circuit to protect it from the effects of lightning.

LITHIUM BROMIDE — a chemical having a high affinity for water used as a catalyst in absorption refrigeration systems

LOCKED ROTOR AMPS — the amperage which is apparent in a live circuit of a motor-driven device when the rotor is not moving

MAKE UP WATER — the water added to a system to compensate for that which was lost during operations

MANOMETER — U-shaped tube used for measuring pressure differences in air passages

MEGOHMETER — an instrument used for evaluating the resistance values of electrical wire coverings

MICRON — one millionth of a meter. 1/25,400 in.

MULLION — a structural bar placed between adjacent doors or windows

NATURAL CIRCULATION — the circulation of fluids resulting from differences in their density

NITROGEN BLANKET — a technique used whereby the air space above a body of water in a vessel is replaced with nitrogen to keep oxygen from coming into contact with its metal surfaces

NOMINAL DIMENSION — an approximate dimension. a conventional size

ONE PIPE SYSTEM — a system in which one pipe serves as both the supply and return main

ORSAT — a device used to analyze gases by absorption into chemical solutions

OVERLOAD PROTECTOR — a safety device designated to stop motors when overload conditions exist.

OXYGEN SCAVENGER — a chemical treatment such as sulfite or hydrazine used for releasing dissolved oxygen from water

PACKAGE BOILER — one that is shipped from the assembly plant completely equipped with all the apparatus needed for its operation

PANEL HEATING — a method whereby interior spaces are heated by pipe coils located within walls, floors and ceilings

PERFECT COMBUSTION — the complete oxidation of a fuel using no excess air for the combustion process

PERIPHERAL DEVICE — a hardware item forming part of a computer system that is not directly connected to but supports the processor

pH — a value that indicates the intensity of the alkalinity or acidity of a solution

PLENUM CHAMBER — a compartment to which ducts are connected enabling the distribution of air to more than one area

POLY-PHASE MOTOR — an electric motor driven by currents out of phase from circuit to circuit.

POSITIVE DISPLACEMENT — an action wherein the total amount of a fluid being transferred by a mechanical device is accomplished without leakage or back siphonage

POTENTIOMETER — a variable resistor in an electrical circuit

POWER FACTOR — an efficiency value assigned to electrical circuits based on a comparison of its true and apparent power characteristics

PRECIPITATION — the removal of constituents from water by chemical means

PRIMARY AIR — combustion air which is introduced into a furnace with the fuel

PRODUCTS OF COMBUSTION — any gas or solid remaining after the burning of a fuel

PSYCHROMETRIC CHART — a graph which depicts the relationship between the pressure, temperature and moisture content of air

P.V.C. — polyvinyl chloride

RADIATION LOSS — the loss of heat from an object to the surrounding air

REFRIGERATION — the removal of heat from an area where it is not wanted to one that is not objectionable

REINFORCED CONCRETE — concrete in which metal mesh or steel bars are imbedded to make it stronger

RINGELMANN CHART — a comparator of smoke density comprised of rectangular grids filled with black lines of various widths on a white background

SATURATED STEAM — dry steam which has reached the temperature corresponding to its pressure

SENSIBLE HEAT — heat which changes the temperature but not the state of a substance

SLING PSYCHROMETER — a device having a wet and a dry bulb thermometer which measures relative humidity when moved rapidly through the air

SPALLING — deterioration of materials evidenced by flaking of their surfaces

SPECIFIC HEAT — a measure of the heat required in Btu's to raise the temperature of one pound of a substance, one degree Fahrenheit. the specific heat of water is 1.0

STATEMENT OF CONSTRUCTION — a document prepared by an architect or registered engineer which elaborates on the fire integrity of a structure

STATIC HEAD — the pressure exerted by the weight of a fluid in a vertical column

STRATIFICATION OF AIR — a condition of the air when little or no movement is evident

TENSILE STRENGTH — the capacity of a material to withstand being stretched

TERRAZZO — a material used for poured floors consisting of concrete mixed with marble chips

THERMOCOUPLE — a device constructed of two dissimilar metals welded together that generates electricity when heated

THERMOSTATIC EXPANSION VALVE — a control device operated by the pressure and temperature of an evaporator which meters the flow of refrigerant to its coil

TON OF REFRIGERATION — the heat required to melt a one-ton block of ice in 24 hours which requires 288,000 Btu's or 12,000 Btu's per hour

UNDERCARPET WIRING SYSTEM — flat insulated wiring designed for running circuits under carpeting where access to wire chases under the floor are not available

UNINTERRUPTIBLE POWER SUPPLY — a separate source of electricity used to maintain continuity of electrical power to a device or system when the normal supply is interrupted

VACUUM — any pressure less than that of the surrounding atmosphere

VAPOR RETARDER — a barrier constructed of materials which retard the capillary action of water into building structures

VELOCIMETER — an instrument used to measure the speed of moving air

VISCOSITY — a measure of a fluid's resistance to flow

WAINSCOTING — any wallcovering that only partially extends from the floor

WET BULB TEMPERATURE — the lowest temperature that can be attained by an object that is wet and exposed to moving air

Index